Uncommon Prayer

Daniel Berrigan

UNCOMMON PRAYER

A Book of Psalms

Illustrations by Robert McGovern

Maryknoll, New York 10545

The Catholic Foreign Mission Society of America (Maryknoll) recruits and trains people for overseas missionary service. Through Orbis Books, Maryknoll aims to foster the international dialogue that is essential to mission. The books published, however, reflect the opinions of their authors and are not meant to represent the official position of the society.

Paperback edition published in 1998 by Orbis Books, Maryknoll, NY 10545-0308.

Originally published in 1978 by Seabury Press.

Manufactured in the United States of America

Library of Congress Cataloging-in-Publication Data

Berrigan, Daniel.
Uncommon prayer : a book of Psalms / Daniel Berrigan ; illustrations by Robert McGovern.
p. cm.
Originally published: New York : Seabury Press, 1978.
ISBN 1-57075-193-5 (pbk.)
1. Bible. O.T. Psalms–Paraphrases, English. I. Title.
BS1440.B55 1998
223'.209505–dc21 98-36585
CIP

To all at Jonah House—
Ed, John
Ledon, Carl
Esther, Barry
Phil, Liz
Frida, Jerry

Life
in the belly
of a paradox

Contents

Introduction

I carry around a dog-eared paperback edition of the psalms, in French, dated 1961. Given the temporal journeys of David's poems, the lives moved, the music put to memory, the monks and their dawn and twilight susurrations, seventeen years is indeed but a drop in a bucket of the well of that fountainhead. Still, in a dry time on earth, it is a joy to return again and again to the psalms. Their waters hiss on the tongue, as though laid against hot metal, or seared flesh. A dry time indeed.

So dry, one asks his soul, are we already in hell, like the rich man who scorned Lazarus? Not yet; we are only on earth, though the distinction between these terrains may someday utterly vanish. Indeed, given the lethal union of violent technology and ruthless diplomacy, the distinction hell-earth may at almost any moment be declared not only irrelevant, but (along with ourselves) obsolete. One thinks in this regard of the sublime triumph known here and there as the neutron bomb, together with the blind pieties which assure us that our arsenals require yet another tinker toy. No matter, if you and I must for some reason perish, our property will survive us intact. On formerly Earth, though the meek will not be around to inherit, the property will be there to testify: who we are, what consummate folly made us the architects of our own doom.

These are somber reflections, admittedly. I can only plead that I did not induce them. The world did, "the way it goes," in Macbeth's phrase. Years and years ago, when I was first introduced to the psalms, my love for them took root in a more or less common assumption: that the world made sense, that lightheartedness and joy were our patrimony, that over and above mere survival, life was a concert, a very conspiracy of hope. That, in consequence, poetry ought to be the ordinary prose of life. And further, that we were to live as long as God does, that death was an interruption, a hiatus, a rude but by no means prevailing wind, knocking us down indeed, but out never.

They have stolen our joy! That is how a biblical indictment of modern life might go. One is not thinking about a snatch of candy from kids. Something horrendous, a very body snatch. We have seen it all; consciousness bent around grotesquely, a wordless cry arising in the void, like a vocalized painting of Guernica. Surely life was not meant to be like this, we cry, so utterly afflicting, weighing us down. And then the question of task, of good work in the world. We think of the classic Christian ideal of "building the earth," of the common assumption of faith: that providence assigns enough for all, a welcome, a network of services and goods for humans. And, above all, no flamboyant death marking us like doomed sticks for the fire, no death as social method, no redundant death, no death by wanton violence, no death outside the course of gentle nature.

I am trying to say (and the saying is difficult indeed) that the vision of humankind, the simple, truthful sense of who we are offered by the psalms, is in principle denied by the spirit and drift of the world today. Denied, violated, put at naught, treated with derision, painted for a fool. Whether this has always been true seems to me beside the point; we are here, and now; and here and now the glory of God is under lethal assault. So is our glory, which is to praise, to invoke, to believe, to live and rejoice in the beloved community. Noting that glory, that dignity, I grew to love the psalms. Day after day, year after year, they purified, blessed, set one moving to a rhythm that was by no means worldly or stereotyped or willful, but lively and tranquil and passionately edgy. To pray the psalms with even half a heart was to be comforted and discomfited, set in motion, set in stillness, set free, set on edge, led outside, led within.

The '60s came on strong, the war hottened up, the psalms went with me into that furnace. I remember saying them in the rubble and bomb shelters of Hanoi, in the Baltimore courtroom, in Danbury prison. There we sat finally (it seemed fairly final at the time), a group of us, stuck fast for the duration. But not so stuck, as it turned out, that we couldn't be set free. The psalms were my freedom songs.

Saying the prayers in prison had a certain piquancy. The psalms were not in the nature of a placebo or a joint (though plenty of both were available, it was a matter of inmate ingenuity or official cataracting). No, in the midst of the sublime public ministries of Nixon and Mitchell et al., the psalms induced a measure of personal balance, created a world of sense and symbol, an underworld of the spirit really, which had in fact always existed (as the psalms said in a hundred ways), a world of humans similar to ourselves, who in the grip of mischance and public violence had undergone God, and lived to sing it out. Heightened knowledge for inert knowledge, rebirth for near death. We needed such moments desperately, to put our clutch on them, like a sinking soul a spar. And then, to let go.

Long before I went to jail, my family and friends had accepted the idea that the scripture, more specifically the psalms, were our landmark, a source of sanity in an insane time. The psalms spoke up for soul, for survival; they pled for all, they bonded us when the world would break us like dry bones. They made sense, where the "facts"—scientific, political, religious—made only nonsense. For me, the psalms gave coloration and texture to life itself; gave weight to silence, the space between words that, like the white in a Cezanne painting, intensify form and color, their other side, a sweet cheat, almost a third dimension.

I began to think, sometime in 1975, all this being so, could I be more precise about my debt, my gratitude?

I decided to try my hand. Not at a translation of psalms, of which there was a surfeit. Rather, to convey a spirit, a way of looking long at the world *sub specie aeternitatis,* looking long at God *sub specie temporis.* The "method," as it developed, hardly deserved so formal a word. It was plain and vagrant, something between letting go and gathering in. I would read a psalm I particularly loved, read it for the nth time, but paying particular attention now to something, a word, a hint, a phrase that caught attention like a hook an eye. It might be a theme, might even, if I were uncommonly lucky, be the point of the original poem. In any case, I went with it; themes like "glory of God," "violence," "suffering," "simple praise," "sorrow," and so forth.

I am entirely responsible for what follows, longing to reach far below the cruel evidence, standing in the muck and fury up to my neck, in the threatened, abused, endangered world, something between a curse and a blessing stuck in my throat—I let it all go.

The prose reflections may be helpful. Some like their poems plain. But, in any case, may the dust of the anonymous early singers and meditators (and the not so anonymous dust of David) not be dishonored in these pages. I feel like invoking those spirits, even their dust. May they stand at our side, for the times are rude, even mad. And do what we may, they are hell bent to worsen. Out of the depths we cry to You.

D.B.

Uncommon Prayer

O Hear My Trouble, Speak Up For Me / *Psalm 4*

Lord, I cower and sweat under a grease paint smile
O hear my trouble, speak up for me

I beat hands bloody on locked doors
windy mouths mouth nothings; lies, the order of day

My teeth grind like a millstone, stuck on the world's grit
circle on circle of nightmare. Awake? Long dead?
I scarcely know. He knows

He reads heart's depth
He stands there, counselor, mighty

"Peace, be silent."
I open eyes, sickened with the age's horror

and meet his face, his face.
Lord, you are joy, are wine

then sing for me, great Vine and vintner and voice
sing out his praise!

We hide our true feelings or dismiss them out of hand. We "manfully" conceal our sorrows. We play-act with those we love. All these, and more—the human equivalent of nature's "protective coloration"?

A fellow prisoner was passing a breakfast tray through the

bars of the D.C. jail. Phil and I were in solitary for dramatizing the graveyard to which our nuclear morticians were consigning us all. The D.C. jail was for some reason not on the list of bicentennial tour stops. You must imagine a foul charnal house, damp, noisy, bug infested; living there is like being stuffed into a tin garbage pail with a mad drummer beating on the lid. After roughly five minutes of your "time," you get the point. You're garbage. You're inside.

Anyway, I said to this trusty, Hope you can smile today, brother.

Said the trusty to me, You can't cry all the time . . .

He was there for a year, without bail, without trial. His real crime never appeared in any indictment; in that invisible cuneiform legible only to cops, judges and wardens it would read: Felon. Convicted at birth. Crime: color, poverty.

Indeed he would die of that stigma, that original sin.

Psalm 4 suggests the terror that produces like a gland secretion, nature's cover. We smile. Indeed, we can't cry all the time! . . .

Thus, a question arises: are we left in that stew, irrevocably drowning?

What does it mean: I open eyes, I meet his face?

I think it means, we don't have to cry all the time. We aren't condemned to be grief ridden, despair ridden. Enduring friendship, undeserved gifts, love of family, love of enemies even—these continue to happen, even to us.

We aren't condemned to go under. The story of rats, roaches, lemmings and other assorted enthusiastically hated or death-driven fauna doesn't exhaust our own story.

There is enough light to go by, at least to take the next step by. There are at least a few people in the world, a precious and steadfast few, before whom we don't have to stand straight, be bloody but unbowed, banish true feelings, play an ironbound part someone else has written for us.

I open eyes, I meet his face. . . . That other one meets us neither as judge, slaveowner, taskmaster, predestinator (he keeps a file on us, he's already made up his mind), prestidigitator (he knows a trick or two, better beware!).

None of these.

And the psalm goes further. This friend is close as the blood of one's own veins, a wine offered us, a vintner holding out his cup. The hint is of something almost forgotten in modern life, something about ecstasy. Unaccountable joy seizing on the heart, a passing moment, a word, even a glance; but a message held out to us. Something as simple, even as banal as, You are not alone. Others understand, love, stand with you.

The moment goes, the word yields silence. And the darkness is darker than ever before. Still, somehow it is relieved, rendered bearable.

The D.C. jail offers the following amenities to its guests: suicides, murders, fires set by maddened prisoners, callous brutalized guards. It is a human bear pit formally dedicated to human destruction.

In the D.C. jail, ecstasy, breakthrough? One must go easy, grace is not a consumer item; many go under.

To his son, God was ruthlessly distant, silent, unreachable. And his conduct remains a scandal, and not only to evil minds. If we believe, he is a scandal to us as well. Often enough, the wine is sour, the vintner sleeps. or so it seems.

There are no claims on God. Except the one that counts. We are his only love.

Who Are We, That You Take Note Of Us? / *Psalm 8*

Through all the universe
your glorious name resounds

I raise eyes
to the lofty tent of the heavens
sun stars moon
foil of your right hand

I see rejoicing
beast and dolphin
eagle, cormorant, condor
triumphant plowing the seas
in the plangent air godlike

I bend to the faces of children
they lisp your name

And I ponder;
mere mortals, who are we
that you
take note of us
have care of us?

fragile, fallible
vermicular, puny—
crowned now, sceptred now
conscious now, exultant now!

Through all the universe
how glorious is your name!

Hand in hand with the degradation of the universe goes the degradation of humans.

Who hasn't seen it? Impossible to destroy the one without losing the other. The community is the universe, grown conscious, its tightest, most fragile center. The community; its roots, outreach, self-understanding, song, art, voice in the world—once broken, bowdlerized, defamed, forbidden—how quickly everything else in the world (including the world itself) goes down the drain!

We seem sometimes to be keeping a death watch at both realities. Our sense of time these days seems like a horrid countdown. The look in our eyes says—if only we can make the next ten years, if only the children have a chance. A new sense of the tragic is everywhere, of the fragility of the world, the fragility of relations among friends and lovers.

Would such fears and dreads possess the heart were it not for the convulsive wars of the past forty years? If the Bomb had never ascended "in clouds of glory," would people not be coping rather well, even today—their sense of themselves enveloped in a sense of providence, of making it in the world?

Hard to say. But one can at least say this: the Bomb is not only the expression of era politics, it is also the nub of our consciousness, the heart of our trouble, the shadow lying heavy on our religious sense.

A totem, a saint's image, a stele, an Easter Island profile, the center of the Stonehenge circle. The Bomb speaks like a monstrous puppet, the voice is our own; our fears, obsessions, hatreds, religious awe, the self-love that breaks us to pieces. It stands for the nuclear character of our consciousness, the breakup, the horror and fear of life together, of a community sense, of a rational parceling out of the goods of the universe.

If the Bomb had not been devised, would we be different people? More human, less prone to hate, more giving, less grasping? In at least one sense, the question is the wrong one. In this sense, being who we are, the Bomb was inevitable. We came first, we hatched that horrid egg, out of our guts, out of our fevered coupling with the powers of darkness. A demon crept out; today it bestrides our consciousness and our world. But before we detonated it, we had fashioned it; and before we had fabricated it, we had dreamed of it. The evil genie arose, not from some ancient jar but from the depths of our own souls.

A song to the glory of God implies that we betray his Name, his Glory, to no idol. Least of all to this one, the god of death.

They Call You Blind Man: Call Their Bluff / *Psalm 10*

Lord, why do you stand on the sidelines
silent as the mouth of the dead, the maw of the grave—
O living One, why?

Evil walks roughshod, the envious set snares
high and mighty the violent ride
Applause for maleficence, rewards for crime
Yourself set to naught

Eyes like a poniard impale the innocent
Death cheap, life cheaper
The mad beast is loosened, his crooked heart mutters
Fear only me!

Lord, they call you blind man. Call their bluff

extinguish their envy

See; the poor are cornered
marked for destruction, grist
for a mill of dust

At the bar of injustice
they tremble, wind-driven birds
under the beaks and stares
of the shrouded Big Ones—
No recourse but you; no recourse
but your faithful love!

The poem is about a collision between rich and poor. And much more.

God is drawn into the imbroglio. For a down-to-earth,

cold-eyed atheism is in the air; as it invariably is, in spite of all pious protestation to the contrary, when the powerful decide to show their hand. The psalm dwells on this point, the difference between faith and incantation, between faith and religious camouflage. On the one hand, the poem celebrates the believing trust of the poor, their spontaneous belief that they will be delivered; and on the other, the neglect, active mistreatment, manipulation, cold-blooded cruelty of those in power.

The conduct of the powerful is almost invariably a mockery of God. Nothing more is required, by way of fulfilling the biblical formula for idolatry, than that the rich be themselves, that is, neglect the poor, live off them, exploit their labor, underpay them, rob them of dignity and hope.

And this sublime, self-deluded charade usually goes on in the midst of the most persuasive cover-up imaginable.

The ultimate deception, of course, occurs in one's own soul, persuaded of the justice of manifest injustice. That achieved, little remains to be done except to institutionalize the lie, introduce it into the structures of public life. Personal crime then flowers in social oppression.

It is at this stage that the oppressor and the prophet collide. A point worth making. In the classical prophets, the attack is mounted not against the personal conduct of the incumbent authority, except insofar as its hypocrisy sets the stage for public injustice. But to the prophet, injustice is the point, invariably, mercilessly. The poor are his passion. Set down, defrauded, shunted about, denied a voice in their destiny, reduced to chattels, to money-making integers, the poor are the occasion, not only of anti-human conduct on the part of their masters, but of atheism, of a non-credo, a denial of God.

Small need to point out parallels today. We are witnessing, on the part of the Nuclear Stokers, a massive, even a cosmic rip-off of the goods of the earth. Land fraud, air fraud, sea fraud, space fraud, food fraud, energy fraud. And now the great apocalyptic super-fraud of them all: the nuclear arsenals, the nuclearization so to speak of all things—of the seas, boundaries, air space, land mass. The nuclearization also of consciousness and experience, defrauding us of our right sense of time and space and one another; of that sense of being reasonably in command, of being sensible co-heirs of the past, cooperators in a human present, co-ancestors of the unborn. Today this ordered, integral understanding of our place in the world is thrown hopelessly out of gear by the Inventive Dwarfs.

Many volumes would be needed to pursue the spiritual damage done us, the destruction of right thinking, by the past thirty years of nuclear mischief. A sense of being correctly centered, of being at ease, at home, rightfully in place in the universe, of being at least potentially brothers and sisters under whatever skies—all this is ruthlessly disrupted. We are nuclear within, we break apart. Any hour might be the last hour. Any stranger might be a terrorist. Irritation is the mood of the times. Any disagreement, even the slightest, provokes us beyond measure; the least provocation can mean a wipeout; an ambiguous move at the frontier, a pricking of our thumbs, the Button.

We conduct our business in the world like a sheriff's bully in a frontier town, our Great Equalizer always at the ready. The Bomb looks out of our eyes; we are literally bombed out. The Bomb has replaced our soul. Near zero point of human hope, near infinity point of human pretention.

In the midst of it all, the church, resplendent and witless, like a cock on a dung heap, salutes the "new dawn." What scene will that dawn bring? What will be left of the good earth? A barren moonscape, a vast cosmic dump? . . .

We may not feel like calling upon God.

We may not feel like calling upon one another.

We may not feel like calling upon our own soul.

We may in fact feel like someone perpetually condemned to walk a Last Mile before execution. Half the horror is getting there.

Or like someone newly dead, still on his feet, going through the robot motions of life. Or like a paraplegic ordered to run the decathalon, or to drag a grand piano across a plowed field, faster than anyone else. To all who live through these or similar nightmares, their daily portion, at least this cold comfort goes out: given the times, such feelings are normal—if anything, they are understated.

Wherefore a group, to be named The Undead Anonymous, is hereby declared in existence. Whose ruling principle is: If you feel dead, waked, buried, disposed of, amortized, the strong possibility is that you are in fact none of these. That you are in fact a dead ringer for the living. Be of good heart. Feeling as you do, undergoing nightmares as you do, you are in a countless company of normal human beings, whose heads are also fogged, heartbeats unsteady, souls shaken. You are alive, you are sane. You should know it.

Prove it to yourself. Make the following simple test.

Call upon God.

Call upon a friend.

Call upon your own soul.

Inquiries invited

Your Word Is Born In Us
Psalm 12

Lord, you have said
murder is forged in the heart, then
slips its sheath: a slip of the tongue
suffices.

Two-faced, the heart turns, turns about
in every wind.
Hot and cold it burns: hot, cold

distempered, twisted,
our willy-nilly constancy

Media drive us mad, demons concoct
on cave walls
their anomie—
announce
like scurrying dwarfs
YOUR DWARFISH FUTURE

voices, a haggle of voices;

guts rumbling like sewers
sewage recycled
[*promises promises*]

And the big thunderers
soul-boggling, superhuman
play to the hilt
the game you never played—

Lies! a theophany of liars
invades, infests the world

Then
germinal, untrammeled
frail as the newborn
your word is born in us

O be
for our sake
midwife to that moment

And when the seventh seal was opened, there was silence in heaven for half an hour. . . .

Once the human story is ended, there is no more need of words. No more need of words! And not of words merely, but of all the sound and fury that passes for human sign, signal, communication. All the noisemaking that seeks to conceal, to stifle the void within, the vast empty yawn of boredom, exhaustion, futility, appetite, moral nausea. This was the way of the world; words issued from words like a polluted spate, a swollen torrent, far back in the watershed of some tainted beginning. Words issued in ever more words, the rivulets join; the headlong stream was empty of substance, mystery; it was disordered, willful, full of menace, helpless to convey or carry the burden of truth.

How grateful we can be in such a world for words which issue out of silence! Silence, the spirit, the fountainhead, eternally self-renewing, giving but never spent, austere but warm of heart, insistent, self-judging, the companion and interpreter of dreams and deeds alike! I remember during the sixties, urging social activists to spend a half hour of silence for every two hours they spent in talk. I have no evidence the advice was heeded. But to me "pure activism" is pure insanity, impossible in fact, a violation of our being, a social monstrosity. . . .

It is not enough to say that at the end of time silence takes over from speech. One must also ponder the question: How about the present? What place is silence accorded here and now?

It is evident first of all that mere talk, even what commonly passes for "expertise," logic, politesse, mere sweepings and parings of the mind, cannot help much; cannot sum up, interpret, strengthen, enlighten our lives. Such talk does not in principle issue from silence. It is merely strung on other talk, former talk, forgotten talk, like bright beads on dull. One can justly say that such palaver issues from nowhere. It comes from a kind of no man's land; a menacing fog-ridden void. Is it any wonder that such words quickly return there, ghosts on the prowl, phantom spies that have learned nothing, taught nothing?

In a culture like our own, words even take on a diabolical overtone. They infest, possess, claim the mind. People actually begin to believe that political claims, advertizing slogans, soap opera scripts, "independent surveys" are telling the truth. Such words, their speakers, their true believers, are drawn into a kind of infernal liturgy, a dance of consumerism, blah politics, worship at the military death shrine.

One notices also how certain words and expressions, well

thumbed, glittering, become a kind of coin of the realm in certain circles. They take on a magical power; they are "in." Woe to the insider who refuses to trade in them, approve them. And woe to the outsider who does not adopt them for his own, does not take up this cause, denounce that one, show himself fervent for the latest imported version of Christianity or Marxism. Voice and vote are denied such a one, he is null and void.

One is reminded of the older view that there are circles also in the inferno, and sub-cultures among the damned. The conduct of many appears, here and now, to prepare for that outcome. There, as often here, power is self-serving, ruthless, efficient as a truncheon; and the powerless are sour as gall. There (as here) hatreds cut across life's possibilities like a grievous fault in nature itself. There (as here) speech is marked by a cynical orotund deceit in the speaker, a cynical disbelief in the hearers.

Electoral politics, right and left; advertising; sermons, commonly; media news, in the main—a guided tour of the inferno. All aboard. Once the tour is over, the tourists take up residence. Last stop, all out. The promise was heaven, the delivery is hell.

Who Enters Your Dwelling, An Honored Guest? / *Psalm 15*

Lord, who enters your dwelling, an honored guest?
Who wins your hand clasp, sister and brother?

The just one, who walks steadfast in truth
whose tongue is a wildfire contained

who sows no dissension abroad
who honors the upright, despises the double deal

who turns the blood of the poor to no base gain
whose word is bond, whose oath is adamant

Behold the Lord's faithful one, sister and brother!

No special word from on high should be needed to answer the question of the psalm: Who enters your dwelling . . . Who wins your hand clasp?

Is this not the genius of a true religious sense, that conduct, conscience and hope dovetail so neatly? One marvel, one being, one improbable height. . . .

In Old Testament and New, to "enter God's dwelling" was an invitation that held the most exalted overtones: communion with the divine, an altogether special friendship, a mystical unity. It is heartening to recall, and salutary as well, that modest, patient, steadfast conduct wins such a reward. Wins it without seeing how, or seeming to deserve it; without indeed expecting it as a just due (which in all truth it is not).

Still, all said, all goodness accomplished, great things are promised!

The just one lives in the light of that promise. His conduct indeed is rightly called an ethic of the promise. The Lord presses upon him and will not be denied. The injustice of the world presses upon him and must be confronted.

A special sense of time is granted such a one; he can be patient without turning to jelly, he knows the cost, the long patience required to bring even a modicum of peace to a savage time, a modicum of justice to the jungle.

Meantime, not everything is crucial, not everything loud is substantial, not everything phenomenal is of the spirit.

The just one lives out this psalm, in all its innocence, directness, modesty. He possesses his soul.

Glory Glory / *Psalm 19*

The heavens bespeak the glory of God.
The firmament ablaze, a text of his works.
Dawn whispers to sunset
Dark to dark the word passes; glory glory.

All in a great silence,
no tongue's clamor—
yet the web of the world trembles
conscious, as of great winds passing.

The bridegroom's tent is raised,
a cry goes up: He comes! a radiant sun
rejoicing, presiding, his wedding day.
From end to end of the universe his progress
No creature, no least being but catches fire from him.

Have you ever felt, for a moment, as though the cruelties of life had receded, shown another face, were tamed, made gentle, a beauty unmarred (for a moment) by habitual savagery?

If we are lucky, such a moment now and again shines from a friend's face, in a flash of love, the errant affection of a child. Or in a moment of solitude perhaps, a mysterious crossing of occasion with place. Or most strangely of all, in a time of agony, loss—suddenly shot through with light. The worst engenders the best; we stand stupefied, trembling with the onset of a mystery that set us reeling, half-killed us, even as it healed.

Such moments! They pull from under us the assurance that we stand on rock. That "routine" is our middle name—our baptismal name even. That a kind of flatfooted shuffle corresponds, in the developed person, to the firm footfall of the pharisee.

Ecstasy is not to be "prepared for," as one cleans out a

room in view of a mysterious guest. Nor is it to be "deserved," as one builds up a bank account to remind him of celestial merits. Nor to be "provided," as country people store apples or turnips against a hard winter.

Everything, all of life converges on that moment—but a hundred lifetimes cannot provoke such a moment, make it happen.

When I am asked, How long did you spend in writing such and such a poem, I answer, fifty-five years and some months. And yet, that said, it remains true that mere fuss and sweat explain nothing. A poem is more than that, ecstasy is more than that. Something more, always something more.

Enjoy! Catch fire from him!

All Day I Cry Out To You
Psalm 22

Eloi Eloi lama sabacthani
My God my God, why have you turned from me?
all day I cry out to you
all night no end to my plaint

But you are silent, are absent
you, the hope of our fathers
the tenderest of mothers
They called out and you answered them
never in vain their half uttered prayer

As for me, I crawl the earth like a worm
a zero, of no account, none.
    The great ones look askance
    their glances pierce me through
    a man made of air

They nudge one another,
palaver behind their hands: there goes the fool
He took his oath to a blank page, he cast his bread
to the dogs, he trampled the law of the land
Now shall God bail him out?

My midwife you were, you drew me
out of the guts of my mother
Red as a budded rose I lay
at your breast and hers
You held me at knee, your first born

My life is pure nightmare
my days are a dance of death
nights a welter of beasts
they circle me, hem me in
(self-concocted, self-sprung
from forehead and groin, my fears
my self-will expended, compounded)
Do I live? I lunge toward death
die? I am cast in the arms of sheol.

My veins run in full flood
my bones are a random fall
my heart melts like a snow
my tongue is a rattling gourd
hands and feet a criminal prey—

crucified to a tree I stand, naked
to mockers. They perch there unblinking
birds of prey
They number my bones
a skeleton sprinkled with lime

O save me my savior! as once you drew me
from the womb of oblivion

bring to a second birth
out of hell's gut, this hapless one.

The ultimate scandal of human life is undoubtedly God himself.

He is the one who sticks in our throats, he it is who offers no relief, who lets the horror of life rampage onward; the great non-interventionist, the great refuser.

This being true, an argument is inevitable. An argument called faith. Biblical faith is just such an argument; it includes a fierce refusal to be turned away, a cry for intervention. Step in! Save! Be yourself, for God's sake!

So the story has gone, from Jeremiah to Job to Jesus—to this day. A questioning faith. Who are you? Who do you say you are? Why must the world go its way, and no one to call a halt? Why the dizzying chasm between your claims and the facts of life? Do not your claims fall before the evidence of history (war, extermination), the common conduct of justice (murder, torture), the common course of diplomacy (nuclear bullying), the common treatment of the powerless (expulsion, starvation)?

Now God could conceivably bear with such impertinences, if they arose from the lips of mere men and women like ourselves, a common run indeed, people by no means enlightened, bereft for the most part of those insights which make of certain great souls his burning glass set to creation, setting all aflame. He could bear with us.

But what is he to make of the tortured cry rising from the lips of his own son, stretched between heaven and earth, testifying with his dying words, not to the interplay of will and will, divine and human, beatitude and earthly paradise; nothing of these. But rather a battle of wills, conducted in a bloody haze, a strange and harrowing love, the father who hearkens but does not intervene, a son whose self-possession forbids that he don the impassive mask of God. A father who loves unto the end, a son who refuses to stare death down, to stonewall his fate in the olympian guise of an "ideal death."

Truly the scandal is God himself. We must not fear being scandalous.

There is a scandal which is the very countenance and look

of faith. There is a scandalous struggle, which is the supreme effort of a son, a daughter to be filial, to be faithful. To be oneself.

Then there is an altogether different scandal, connected not with faith but with faithlessness. Jesus confronted it also; hypocrisy, empty observance, self-serving, religion by rote. Such pseudo-scandal, it goes without saying, ends up neither on the cross nor in conflict with God. Nor in friendship with God.

"Today if you hear his voice, do not harden your hearts . . ."

I Look For Him Who Looked For You / *Psalm 23*

You keep on nudging me, mostly in dreams—
keep on keeping on! seek my son David
he has clues, clues

I look for him who looked for you;
footprints like a fossil of fern
shadow of a hand

on a bone lyre. Next to nothing.
What are those "clues clues" you keep
insisting on?

arrow heads point toward a shore
a skeletal sun boat, waters ingathered
like tears spent or misspent; or Lethe crossed
when the raft is the shore.

Not "what clues"; but "clues of what"
scout or shepherd, David had asked.
Ask! you urge, nudge.
Is that why
the bone lyre curves like a question?

Not "what clues" but "clues of what."

In the poem, David the poet is also a kind of scout, a spy even. He goes ahead of others, secretly takes soundings, reports back on the terrain.

The image is not one of seeking out the future; more like one exploring an unknown land. Earth creatures we may be, but after so long a time we know very little of the lay of the land—even our own.

We don't know ourselves, we don't know one another, we want a wisdom we only succeed in reading about in old books or hearing about, the wisdom of remote endangered tribes. The wisdom is as strange to us, as esoteric, as the costumes, the paint and feathers, the nakedness.

We know facts, mountains of facts; whole Himalayas stand there inert. We are ignorant of the clues; we can't read the signs. The difference is a notable one, a dolorous one; we attack problems voraciously when the (invariably) scientific mood takes us. Then the fires are kindled—curiosity—and the witch's brew bubbling. But mysteries! We defame them, blithely ignore them, walk roughshod over them. Mystery! What's that?

About a civilized life, which begins, one would think, with mutual acceptance, peaceableness, a gesture across a street, across the world—we haven't a clue. Or rather we had one, but it died of neglect.

One thinks of buckets of spilt blood, multiplied horrors, our rake's progress across the world's face—exploration, exploitation.

One thinks also of the resolute saints in our midst, prophets, scouts, clairvoyants in the difficult matter of clues. They came, they keep coming among us with a simple resolve, to read things right, to tell the truth. Their blood, in consequence, invariably flows, whole buckets of blood; their bones are pressed into the road bed; over them the Big Ones careen.

David's question was a good one; he did not ask "what clues?" but "clues of what?" He did not want to stop along the way, taking the clues of god for God himself. He asked to be led further. He wanted to be something more than a collector, avaricious, grasping, edgy; a collector of religious wonders, of the miraculous, of gaudy interventions.

May we not think in this regard of a kind of sanitized superstition; of people who pursue, bully verbally, corner, argue, put others on the spot (are you reborn? in the spirit?).

Such, to be sure, work a blight on language; they literally boggle the mind. The language is forced, a blunt weapon; so it becomes its own opposite, profoundly irreligious, disharmonious, out of place, somewhat like a lovely child dragged through foulness. The setting is wrong, the clues are stolen from their proper environs, biblical rebirth becomes a kind of bloody abortion; the joy, sting, sharp savor, primary weather of experience are gone.

Collecting versus expending. I had rather a hundred times spend my life's energies working to heal the injustice around me, and never once speak of God; of doing it for God, of clarifying my motives(!)—than spend life converting others to God, while I gave not a snap for prisoners, slave camps, wars, starving peoples, the sins of the mighty. To what God would I be converting others, in such a demented case? In what God would I believe?

In the first example, it seems to me that the clues are seen for what they are, signs to be led by. The injustices of the world, the harrowing of hell, the victimized crushed faces, the implacable half-smile of judges, all life's edgy necessities—all of these urge us on. Into the world, into service of God, who bleeds there, is defeated and degraded there.

In the second case, the clues are dead, stony, empty shells. The world says nothing to me, it has nothing to say. It is cruelly silent, inert, cyclic, a turning cage. Nothing can be done for people, against tyrants.

The lyre on which David played I take as symbol of true

understanding. Like a bone on a shore, it leads further, it entices, teases the mind—outward, across. A bone—of what, of whom? The lyre "curves like a question," a clue. A clue of—what?

If I seize on the clue, collect it, take possession of it, I lose it. If I leave it alone, leave it there, raise my eyes in the direction it curves toward, then I get somewhere. I embrace the question its very existence raises. Whom did David sing of? When will I see the face of God?

People, events, baleful structures, the burden of living consciously, the sixth sense that makes one furious at needless suffering (and keeps one furious, and proud of that fury), a sense of proportion (not too big for the world, not so elated by praise that I can't bear a putdown), ability to be silent and listen—clues, beckonings onward. If we are faithful to these, the hidden face will turn to us. On a day we can neither predict nor bring to pass.

I cannot command the sun to rise. I know it will rise. Tomorrow; in your light we will see the light.

The Trusting Heart Shall Prevail
Psalm 31

How great is your goodness Lord
poured out on the one who loves you
Face to face with iniquity
the trusting heart shall prevail

Far from intrigue, from malice
I run to your presence, take sanctuary
in your eyes. Hands aloft, you encompass
a holy tent, a refuge.

The war of tongues, a babble, a rout
rages, goes nowhere.
I would dwell
tongue stilled, mind subdued
in your holy temple

Come, make me your temple
deep founded, touching high heaven

All you who fear the Lord
exult, take courage
come shelter in him!

The beauty of the psalm is in the mouth of the speaker, murmurer, singer, pray-er. The beauty, the wonder, is that we can say the psalm—with all our heart. The trouble is, we have no roof to say it under.

Someone wrote of the Catholic radicals, they have no trouble with the church as such; their trouble is with current leadership. Exactly. And well put, as far as it goes; but what is one to do when the leadership "carries on" with a war establishment, when the Vietnam scandal becomes the post-Vietnam scandal? And this scandal is so nearly universal among the authorities that some of us, for sanity's sake, must stay out in the cold. Outside. Willy-nilly, this is what it has come to—for years and years now.

But you keep on keeping on, praying. The nub: faithlessness on our part is no response to dereliction on theirs.

They held an enormous mass in Philadelphia during the eucharistic congress; the date was August 6, 1976. They held a mass to honor the military forces of the world. That was the unutterable scandal, the blasphemy. They dared say the Lord's prayer, Remember me, which bring his saving death to our life. And they forgot. It was not merely that they forgot what date it was, Hiroshima Day. Deeper, beyond deep, in the dark where dry bones lie where they fall. They forgot. They celebrated not His death, but death. It was not a mass, it was blasphemy. And not a mere handful took part, as though some protested, but all who came to the congress, and several cardinals. That church in procession walked stately toward an altar. And they fell off the edge of the world.

Other Christians stood outside. It was a very old story. Fasting, offering leaflets concerning this weighty matter, this sin of commission (a military commission), this sin of omission, of forgetting, of omitting to be the church.

It was another sorrow in a litany of sorrows. Another lesson (we are slow learners), yet another, in a whole education, years and years in the benches saying to ourselves, No, they can't mean that; or, You probably misunderstood; or, I'll come back next week, things are bound to get better. . . . After a long time, even the retarded (myself) should have known.

Your optimism sounds, even in your own ears, more and more like a graveyard tactic, with a difference. You whistle, but you hang around the grave. Now it is over. No more whistling, no more hanging around.

Which is not to be taken as meaning: No more leafletting, no more standing there, no more fasting, no more speaking the truth. Quite the contrary.

But what has all this to do with psalm 30?

It's a matter of architecture, of tone, of the place the soul desires, thirsts for, hungers for, wants to kneel in; a matter also of faces, Catholic faces, and being able to preach and shrive and bless and give holy bread away. A matter of access, of connection. Of leaving many things, growing out of many things—but never out of the one Thing. A matter of not being literally out in the cold. Of not having to recite a psalm meant to be recited in chorus, in community, in a sacred place—not being forced to recite it, having to summon more faith, a greater faith, than the psalm asks for; which is simply that it be said by believers together in a believing way.

But now the prayer must be said alone, or at least outside. That is the deep wrong, that is awry, that should not be. And for years and years. Where they cannot persecute, they ignore. And thus life goes.

This little psalm, so ingenuous, such a childlike burst of love, opens more life than one can easily bear.

I do not mean to leave it at that. For there are other matters too, not all of them sombre; other consolations, other friends. We must hold our hands high over one another, forming a living sanctuary, our protection and canopy, a sacred space, though a sorrowful one.

Let us say the psalm with compassion, for those outside, because their conscience is granted no place inside.

Let us say the psalm, also with compassion, for those who honor violence, and summon to that dishonor the meek and peacemaking Lord. And themselves, and us as well.

Tell Me The Way / *Psalm 32*

I keep my eyes peeled, alert to your nod

but there's a balky horse in my head
a backward jackass braying

only bit and bridle
will bend this two-way will your way

Come then, unmuddle me, master me!

Loud, clear, tell me the way to go.

Because I do not know the way
because you have said, I am the way
because the way is obscured by a thousand detours, wrong turns, deceiving signs. Each of them marked One And Only

because with all my intemperate heart I want to arrive here
and now but must go on; to there, to then
because of duty and law and responsibility and obligation
and so on and so on; how I weary myself (and undoubtedly you)
and lose your gracious gesture, and tie myself in knots
because "law" is a cover for my lawlessness, not the freedom
you offer
and "duty" gets along with my deviousness
and "obligation" is hand in glove with my laxity
and "responsibility" is a cover for childishness.
So I carry about these heavy absurd words, a beast's burden
because in fact I wish to be burdened, dread to be free
which is to say, I dread to be your friend and brother.
Nevertheless
now and again your word reaches me
What moments those are!
everything stops short, as between heartbeats
A strange joy, as though my face were touched and held by
two hands
as though an egg split in two, and I stood there, born for a
change; alive for a change
utterly changed (for a change)
Then, of course, my old demons return; or as they say, life
goes on
which is to say, and closer to the fact
death goes on
except that death does not quite go on, not in the old way
not altogether calling the plays.
Those moments of grace! like an arrow of sunlight
along a mausoleum floor
Something is happening, the door must be slightly ajar
I have a name for you; you are
the crack of light
under the door
of the city morgue.
Any minute now I may hear my name called: Lazarus.

Into His Right Hand / *Psalm 33*

SECURITY SECURITY, the plain chant of the damned.
Border guards, guard dogs, gun sights
an investiture of death. Yet

what is so vulnerable as we,
who cave in at a blow
who fall like kicked sacks?

we die in an hour, insects, flowers
we drift down wind, we are shadows in armor
death our portion, our menu, our bleak house;

And the God of life? he took clay
like a master potter, heart shaped clay
fired it with his breath. And we stood there

children, people, animals, insects and flowers.
The diurnal planets
he set spinning on his fingertips, let them go
Like a feather, down wind.

> *See, brutes huff and puff*
> *they rake the world with fire*
> *they build hecatombs*
> *of shuddering bones*
>
> *The Lord of life*
> *keeps them at edge of eye*
> *half attentive*
> *no need of his*
> *vengeance, judgment;*
> *they crumble like a*
> *faulty tower*
> *down wind*

at center eye
the apple of his eye
blossoms, swells, ripens
—the faithful who fall
straight as a plumb line
into
his right hand.

"Everybody wants to go to heaven, but nobody wants to die."

I see America building a fortress of temporal beatitude where death is banished. Death is outside in the dark, immortality within. So goes the myth, the diseased hope; it is reinforced with concrete, radar, sonar, nuclear bunkers, with every brooding death-dealing device imaginable. Death is to be inflicted on others, at the drop of an insult, the tiniest provocation. But death is never to be suffered by the happy inventors and investors of immortality.

Of course, things don't work out exactly as planned. The big guns ricochet, the nuclear wastes seep out like bad news, the winds drift back unexpectedly, death is pollen on the air. Inexplicably, too, in the air within the Fortunate Fortress, a masque is in progress, a revel; but it turns sour. People keep meeting peoples' eyes; they read panic there, bewilderment, despair. What is happening to us?

Now the music begins to wail; it sounds more like a dirge than a ball. The floors rock, the night turns to a demented rout. Nothing holds; the fortress is built on an earth fault. The earth opens.

The Bible speaks of God's sense of time—or of timing. The kingdom of a thousand years falls in an hour. The violent pretentions of the powerful turn to a whimper, fire rains down, the proud builders of empire flee, hide out in bunkers, cower there in the dark. They were ignorant, blind as bats from the start. Illiterate, too, for all their posturing before history's mirror, their napoleonic braggadocio. Their stance was cowardly. Their destiny is a bore.

Immensely more to the point here, of more interest to a

human future, is the fate of the just. Human rights, honor, work, a human future, were as often as not denied them; they were the losers, defeated, brought down. Their refusal of violence was their undoing, the outcome was as simple as it was brutal. The machine of the world crushed them.

Or so it seemed.

That it only seemed so, that another outcome took place, is the theme of the psalm.

Which is to say: the just were (are) the seed of a new creation; the building blocks, indeed the builders, of the new Jerusalem.

Here and now living among us, or remote, long lead, only heard of, read about—such persons give us hope in a nearly hopeless time. Where else but from them do we draw sustenance, to hold firm against the cult of violence, hatred, the grinding duplicity that consumes us?

The psalm should be read, it seems to me, in conjunction with the words of Jesus about good and evil in the world, tares and wheat flourish together in the fields until harvest time. This is a summons to patience and the withholding of judgment.

God is judge, the just are patient. They are patient under the withholding of justice, under manifest injustice.

Patient also, with God.

Make My Heart Over / *Psalm 39*

Behold your son of excellent intentions!
I said to my soul:
set guard
to your tongue—
nothing, no one
take you by surprise.

How little I reckoned!
my heart erupted
anger possessed me, vortex and demon.
The impious took aim.
I fell like a ninepin.

Shamed I walk now

Healer, lover
who will make whole
that pure intent
that eye of single desire?

make my heart over

St. James the apostle, who was not one to mince matters, has a red hot message to the church, mostly about anger; but in any case, about old fashioned "sins of the tongue."

> The tongue is like a fire. It represents in our bodies the world with all its wickedness. It pollutes our whole being; it keeps the wheel of our existence red hot, and its flames are fed by hell.
>
> Beasts and birds of every kind, creatures that crawl the ground or swim in the sea, can be subdued, have been subdued. But no one can subdue the tongue. It is an intractable evil, charged with deadly venom.
>
> We use the tongue to sing the praises of our Lord and God, and we use it to curse our fellows, who are made in God's likeness. Out of the same mouth come praises and curses.
>
> My friends, this should not be so. Does a fountain run with fresh and brackish water from one spout? Can a fig tree yield olives, or a vine figs? No more does saltwater yield fresh. . . .

One wants to let it go at that, a kind of last word about bad words. A question remains though, especially about words of anger.

Are such always and everywhere forbidden?

Always and everywhere is too easy, especially when one thinks of Jesus and his response to hypocrisy, double dealing, rotten religion, defrauding of the poor, the dishonoring of his Father's house.

Difficult matters. We can trace anger back and back in history, through the prophets, back to Cain's inflamed heart; and murder. Good and ill. Instrument of justice, instrument of hatred, two fused metals, two edges of one blade, anger.

How can one live in the world today, with eyes open, and not be angry? It seems to me impossible, spiritually, humanly. It goes against the grain of the soul; always to be equable, and yet to be conscious. No, anger is a fire in the mind; it gives light to go by, heat, energy.

And yet it seems to me that anger cannot be the main business of life, if life is to go anywhere. The question to be put: is our anger in service; is it the warmth, the quality, the preserving element of our passion for justice, of our love for others?

Keep the flame going, but low; burning, but not burning up.

The Lord Is Lord, Our Refuge, Our Strength / *Psalm 46*

Mountains topple, streams halt in their tracks
Earth flushes and pales, storm upon calm pell mell
Time traces, retraces its steps like a sleepwalking sentry

No matter. The Lord is Lord, our refuge, our strength

There's a river I know of: in its arms
the city of God rests secure.
Turmoil, unrest, a fevered succession of powers?

No matter. The Lord is Lord, our refuge, our strength.

He breaks in its socket the fiery fasces of war
arrows and lances, rockets, obscene machinations
the idols we make he unmakes, false gods, cheap salvation

Rejoice. The Lord is Lord, our refuge, our strength.

We will never outgrow these hymns, songs, prayers. They take the world into account, with a sure hand, hold it to an accounting. Ourselves.

The prayers are worldly, in the best sense, they know the world, its ways, its wars, its crooked heart; they apply to its wounds a superior wisdom. Sing away old monks, pray, pray old believers, sweat it out, this fever and chill called life!

The prayer is inclusive, a different thing than being accepting. The storms, the natural disasters, torrid season and freezing. And then that disaster above all natural measure and scope. Named—ourselves. The psalms must include us; our skill in fashioning catastrophes above and beyond those in nature, surpassing them all.

Let us pray the psalm for all who die in war, the supreme unnatural humanly sponsored disaster of them all.

Let us pray for all who learn nothing from the history of war, and rush forward perfervedly into new ones.

Let us pray for those who make peace, and pay its cost with stout hearts.

Let us pray also for those millions trapped in the great web of war diplomacy, war research, war production, arms sales, arms buying. For all who make their living through others' dying.

Let us pray for good taxpayers, good citizens, people of law and order, good Christians. That they awaken from their sleep. For sisters, priests, monks, scholars, that passion inform their minds, compassion their discipline. Not merely hearers, but doers of the word.

Let us not weary of praying. Nor of speaking and acting. While there is yet light. . . .

There is a cult, an idolatry of action. There is an idolatry, a cult of prayer. The first is a mad escape, the second a consumer item, a narcotic. (It was no coincidence that the druggies in prison with us were all great meditators.) Each taken alone, activism, passivism, without the other, is hardly recognizable as a human activity; the activists grow sour, violence prone; the meditators dwell on the moon, lunar.

The question is not merely one of integrating these two. The question is how to recover each of these two, shapeless, defamed and lost; meaningless action, pointless prayer.

Let us pray, finally, for those who act and for those who pray. For those who act prayerfully, as though in love; for those who pray in view of an act to come; an act of love, even of heroic love.

The great words of James the apostle come to mind. (A letter seldom heard in the churches.) Let us make of it our prayer, a prayer that will heal, unite, restore us to ourselves, to one another.

What use is it for one to say, I have faith, and then do nothing to show that faith? Can such a faith save? Suppose a brother or sister stands there in rags, hungry. And one of you says, Good luck, may you have food and clothing to spare, and then passes by. What is the good of those good wishes, and nothing done to supply a need?

So it is with faith. If it leads to no action, it remains dead as a doornail.

But maybe someone will object: That's well and good, but it takes all kinds. Some point to their faith, others to their deeds, they seem satisfied. . . .

Look, show me how this standstill faith can be real, and I'll show you how faith is at the heart of my good works.

Well, you say, of course I believe; I believe in one God. . . . So do the demons; they believe and tremble. Believe away, quibble away. But know it in spite of yourself, faith without action is barren, a stone, a corpse.

My Plenty, My Harvest / *Psalm 53*

The madman said in his heart
God is dead.
Earth shook! a trumpet blast, a bell's
fiery throat

And God walks his world
a guru in rags
lamp in hand, everywhere seeking
one face of trust

Here, there, on this side and that,
trembling, anticipant—
Where his light falls, eyes avert, shadows fret
a congress in hell
a herd at the abattoir, stupefied, sweating
No just one, not one!

The feast is set. A beggar at door
lamp snuffed, pinchbeck face—
Clamor within; bones break, blood spills
a cannibal feast

Faces malign, insolvent, grotesque. The beggar
takes wing like a swallow
High on the wall a judgment appears
"mene, teqel, parsan"
—found wanting!
—rejected!
—replaced!

Blood-gorged, they sink in a welter of blood.
The bones of the just
arise, a wheat field serene

God walks in their midst
"My myriad just ones
my plenty, my harvest."

The psalm speaks of a cannibal feast presided over by the great ones of this world. The menu: the body and blood of their victims.

If the imagery seems atrocious, let us meditate on verse 5 of the original psalm.

> Will all these evildoers never learn,
> they who eat up my people like bread,
> who refuse to call upon God?

As well as this scene from the book of Revelation, chapter 19:

> And I saw an angel standing in the sun, and he cried with a loud voice, saying to all the birds that fly in mid-heaven, come, gather together for the great supper of God, that you may eat the flesh of kings, the flesh of officials, the flesh of the mighty, the flesh of horses and of those who sit upon them; the flesh of all, free and slave, small and great.

Where else does consumerism end, especially that consuming act par excellence, war, but in cannibalism?

And what sort of god do the warmakers cherish after all, and desire with all their fleshly hearts, but a flesh-eating god? A god, that is to say, created in their own image, tongue to gullet to anus.

For this reason the nightmares of Revelation are exactly that: an unclouded mirror of our own voracious souls, a nightmare of appetites on the hoof, a will to make of the world and its peoples a hellish banquet, an ultimate anti-eucharist at which the honored guest will be the anti-Christ—violent, self-honored, self-damned, ourselves.

The nightmares of scripture are our most secret, guarded, cherished dreams turned inside out, taken up by God, and tossed back at us: fast food for the damned.

Do we quail, do we ask in hurt wonderment, what kind of God would speak like that, act like that? Let us consult our own heart for answer, the dark demons infesting us, the urges that assume the force of commands, the gods enthroned there, sinister, in control.

With this for prelude, the imagery of the psalm seems, if anything, rather subdued. God walks the earth, a Greek patriarch, a wandering Jew, a Russian holy man, in search of justice. He comes to a princely home where an unholy banquet is in progress. The imagery of the handwriting on the wall is derived from the book of Daniel, chapter 5. The crime mentioned in Daniel is a double one: idolatry and theft of the holy vessels. In the psalm, in line with Revelation, the crime is cannibalism. I see no great difference. In any case, the punishment is too close for comfort: the end of our era, our lives weighed and found wanting, our kingdom divided.

Our Karma Is Near / *Psalm 58*

The brahmins enter
dressed to kill
ermine and periwigs

sober as mourners
mouths like the grave
"justice their errand"

Crooked in spirit
skilled in deceit
merciless of tongue

they stop their ears
lest they be chastened, shed
of their venomous ways

Then fall on them, vengeance!
break their bones
open their veins
Off the earth's face with them
aborted, inhuman
grant them no light of day!

Tempests carry them off
root, branch and thorn!

The joy of the just is this;
an end of injustice.
He exults, he washes his limbs
in the blood of the wicked

Shout it; our karma is near!
mockers, God is not mocked!

I yield to no one in my fascination with law courts. Indeed, to only a few in my frequent attendance upon them.

A decade ago, the foregoing sentence could hardly have been composed, except perhaps in the throes of high fever. We clerics were as innocent of the law in action as we were of lawlessness in action. And the idea that the two could be conjoined—that the law could be lawless—that was a secular blasphemy that could never have crossed our lily lips.

Alas, the times change. The war brought many of us to the bar . . . of justice, they said. Inevitably, we began to taste the justice meted out to the poor, the bewildered, the broken, those whom one or another circumstance, usually beyond their control, poverty or race, dumped at birth outside the law. From then on their biology was their fate. It was as simple as that. A lethal simplicity; on the faces of judges it came out in a black mix of boredom and malice.

Well, we were hailed into court too. When we appeared, the boredom vanished, the malice intensified. It was like a recognition scene in hell; the priest you had last seen at the altar you now saw in the dock. Something was dragged down, something was soiled. It could not be borne with, the ironies tightened. A priest, commissioned by his sacrament to sit in judgment, was now sat upon, in judgment. The judge who, at other times, in other places, had knelt at the priest's hands for forgiveness, now waved the priest away into durance vile. Who held the keys of the kingdom now? Who rattled these keys fiercely and would even strike out with them, against this transgressor, this soiler of a holy office, if judicial decorum did not forbade anything but a storm cloud of black looks?

It was a reversal, a turnabout, an irony, a dramatic shake-out of one's very seams. It was worthy of Greek drama; it was even worthy of the gospel, at least in the sense that it brought to life many of those stage instructions issued by the Lord for the final drama. Truly, in court, the first were now last, the master was servant, the ungarmented (more literally, the defrocked) were cast in darkness. We tasted what we had taught, some of us glibly, for many years. The gospel. It had been sweet as honey on our tongue, it was bitter as gall in the guts. . . .

I have had to ask myself whether such a terrifying psalm as this one (58) belongs in a book of devotions. What has such anger, such an outcry, so fierce a sense of outrage, to do with prayer to God?

Then I came to see . . . everything. In the first place, because the same, or at least an equivalent poem, festers away in the book of psalms. Why there, unless it speaks truly, irreplaceably even, of our plight—as indeed does any other psalm? And is this cry of outrage not approved and blessed by the fact of being there in scripture?

I thank God with all my felonious heart that the poem is not my own, but a psalm; not merely a word from us to him, but, more to the point, from him to us.

Which leads to another reason for gratitude and inclusion. Nonviolent lawbreaking—courts, jails—have been a part of our existence (mine, my brother's and friends') for at least a decade now. The necessity is still there, an unhealed wound; our country continues to concoct and purvey death, violence, war. Like a corpse in electric spasm, America lurches this way and that, hot war to cold, horrifying mock gestures of life, but never life itself. A life which my faith would long to translate: peace. But there is no peace.

Therefore we resist. We will not be kept alive by murderous infusions of others' blood, like some stalking Dracula.

Therefore this poem meets our experience, even as we continue to be hailed before judges. Wicked, some of them; enlisted, all of them. Therefore, with now and again a fit or start of compassion or understanding, always roughly the same outcome. Guilty. And sentenced.

Even as I compose this prayer, hoping to be faithful to the spirit of the original, I pray as well as I might that malice, hatred, bitter memory in the mind, have not seized on me. If the poem is here, in these pages, let it be only because it was first there, in the book of Psalms.

When you read it here, please do so meditatively; and compare it with the original, in whatever language. I believe it is faithful.

A further question arises. Beyond a diatribe against unjust judges, what meaning can the psalm bear? What word does it bring from God to those who will never, for any reason, stand before judges?

At least this. Every human court is a prelude to final judgment. Imperfect, sometimes murderously unjust; often presided over by a hanging judge morosely conducting a kangaroo court. But even at its best, when its justice reflects a just society, the court is still only a dim image of things to come: the justice of a God who reads the heart, in all its murkiness, unease, fits and starts.

It is good to reflect on this. Courts are by and large whipping posts where victims get whipped. The vast majority of courts, in any society, have only the faintest connection with justice, law, order. Rather, they mirror, with a great waste of huffing and puffing, the injustice, lawlessness and disorder which are the law of survival in the jungle at large. Their pompous ceremony is for the most part a front; behind the elegant paneling, the flags, robes, venerable faces, the dead furniture of law; behind all this, there stretches a bridge of sighs, and beyond that, a dungeon. Its inhabitants are literally off the human map; they are nonpersons. Meantime, out front, the theater of cruelty goes on; the principals cavil, split hairs, cite texts, stroke their egos, justify, as best they might, high crime; better, low crime in high places. And of course, punish the witless, the ignorant and the innocent.

For Americans, our psalm may be salutary. It penetrates the foggy aura which, in our cataracted eyes, surrounds the law and its functionaries. They can do no wrong! How could they? For if they did, were we not wrong also, our witless awe misplaced, our childish trust violated?

No, the psalm offers no comfort to debased, secular, savage, economically sound, law and order. It urges us to look narrowly at the courts, to consider the racism, narrow vengeance and cupidity which so often energize and inflame the law, turnings its blade in one direction only.

God has turned the sword another way; he has grasped its handle himself. The psalm is a judgment poured out, not on the accused, not even on the convicted. It is a judgment on the judges.

Then we look on the accused (the one who speaks in the psalm). He is under fire. Punishment hangs heavy over him. But one thing remains; he is capable of rage, his spirit is unbroken. His burden is his innocence. He cannot lighten it or cast it off. So he cries out to God, redeemer, savior, just judge.

It goes without saying that a totally different sort of prayer than this psalm would arise to the lips of most Christians whose lives touched on the law courts. Most could compose a heady prayer on behalf of judges and prosecutors, would call on a God of law and order to maintain order in the court, to protect the law of the land. No matter that such a god is the God neither of the psalmist nor of the prophets, nor of Jesus himself. Enough. He is our god, let him care for our interests, vested and invested. Amen.

The amen is presumptuous. While we and the judges and the police and the prosecutors and the jury conspire together, summon their god, adjure him to attend their cause, who is that ragged figure shivering in the dock, forever under fire, at the edge, unkempt, unacceptable? Let his own words speak for him. I have come to summon not the just, but sinners; they will enter the kingdom before you.

Show Me Your Face, O God
Psalm 61

At land's end, end of tether
where the sea turns in sleep
ponderous, menacing
and my spirit fails and runs
landward, seaward, askelter

I pray you
make new
this hireling heart
O
turn your face to me
—winged, majestic, angelic—

tireless,
a tide
my prayer goes up—
show me your face, O God!

Turning about, in human affairs, seems to be fair play. Doesn't the scripture have it so, and the gospel hymn—Turn, turn, turn . . . ?

A twist rather than a turn, open-field running, evasions, excuses, ifs. Our lives go this way. But should they? Can this be what scripture is recommending? If one were to judge by

the performance, among ourselves, such would seem to be the fact. Or, at least, so an outsider would judge: behold how these Christians evade one another.

Still, something other than a way, multiple ways out, would seem to be at issue. Out of responsibility, out of sorrow and conflict, out of the repeated melancholy failure of good things, of high hopes, of trust placed squarely, at great cost, in others.

Then: inertia, paralysis, that indifference more damning than hatred, more corrosive than fury. Turnabout is unfair. "O turn your face to me!" Was there ever a more beautiful prayer, a gentler reminder to Him that He, as well as we, and with a more terrible outcome than ours, wears a human face? And that a quality, a mark of the human (perhaps the highest mark) is that one turns to another when a cry for help is raised? And since He is divine, will He not for that very reason be more intensely human? And therefore will He not hear more acutely, respond more quickly, be attuned to such a cry as we raise, as indeed our very lives continually raise?

I have heard a mother or father suddenly interrupt a conversation, sit stock still listening. A child was crying in the house, awakened perhaps from sleep. I marveled, for I had heard nothing. We ask Him to turn His face to us. He has heard. He is parent, brother, mother, friend.

We cannot turn to Him first. Indeed our very crying out is by His grace. How else put the matter? This is a very old dispute and contention. But among Christians it was settled long ago. We are dead men and women, the dry bones of Ezekiel's desert, until He quickens us. This is our true nature and state, and our saving self-knowledge is to know it: that we are dead, doomed, until He turns to us.

He has already done so; or we would not have cried out to Him to do so. We love that hope. We hope for that love.

A Mercy, A Healing / *Psalm 64*

I walk in your world
a mercy, a healing—

Like a cooper of barrels
you bind the mountains with ribbing
your hand rests on rambunctious seas
they grow peaceful
the brow of a sleeping child

Autumn is a king's progress
largesse lies ripe on the land

up, down the furrow your midas touch
ruins gold;
rainbows arc from your glance

Fall of rain, evenfall, all all is blessing!

A hymn of joy for the unity of the visible world! A unity that sacrifices nothing, a unity neither uniform (as though the world were some sort of grim Iron Mountain) nor chancy ("everything thrown in the air falls somehow together").

The marvelous unity of the world. A delicate balance, a balance of oppositions, a mutual respiration, glow, decline, rebirth. Perhaps we begin to sing its praises only when it is in danger, when our denial or violation of the world's integrity endangers our own sweet existence.

Is this not the situation today? The cosmic unity, a network of biological interplay, makes all living beings parts of the bead game of life. And yet, and yet. Despair and destructiveness, cupidity, have literally declared war on creation.

One marvels at this hardening of spirit, a blindness that allows the mighty ones of this world—statesmen, engineers, tacticians, experts in applied and physical sciences—to contemplate with calm the destruction of our race, of the visible world, of all life. Their scheme, ineffably militarized, untouchably abstract, goes by various names; "preemptive first strike, MIRV, MARV, MAD."

These cosmic vandals would have the splendid universe, with its hard won victories of spirit over ego, conscience over instinct, culture over technique, love over violence, all reduced in a few moments to one dead level of dust and rubble. And all in the name of some ideology, as primitive as it is obscure; a fracas of east vs. west, a long, drawn out blood-letting, a test of nerve, an irresistible movement of both sides toward some mad showdown.

Such insanity has outrun our dictionaries, our ethics handbooks, our moral maps and charts, our health skills. We have no capacity to deal with it. Who will shed light on a deathwish that includes in its mad outreach all humans, all life, the earth itself? Psychiatry, religion, history of nations and tyrants? The experts drop their arms, they shrug helplessly.

We have seen Eichmann in the dock, we have seen three domestic presidents endorsing, commanding, concealing war crimes in Asia. Earlier we heard Truman, eyes cold as death, announcing the wipeout of two Japanese cities. Years later he died in his own bed and was buried honorably. There is no reason to believe he was troubled in his Christian conscience about the unutterable crime of that August day.

Today, by no means out of countenance, the restless parricides speculate, doodle, put out feelers, create incidents, inflame and narcoticize the public—then actually produce their next infernal infant, named B-1, named Trident. The brain children, it is announced, both swim and fly. Hounds of hell, hungry for human meat, their noses point one way. The day they long for, the day they bring nearer, is named Doom.

All of which leads one to reflect on kinds of unity other than that of the physical universe. There is also a mysterious moral unity joining us, one to the other, will to will, person to community, nation to nation, the living to the unborn and the dead. The links are forged of adamant; they join us irrevocably in mutual guilt and innocence, in accountability and judgment. There is no escaping this bond; it will be honored or it will have its revenge. It is as implacable and blind as the law of gravity.

What revenge pursues those who sunder this unity? The Bible speaks of a plague of moral blindness and lets it go at that, as though the illness were its own punishment, as indeed it is. We recall with a kind of awe, almost a sense of fear, how Jesus passed by certain individuals of his own time. He was silent before them, he granted them not a moment. His scorn was both subtle and stunning. They were blind, he said, incurably blind. Their feet were set toward damnation, a turnaround was literally impossible, like the squaring of a circle, self-contradictory, far less imaginable than the raising of the dead.

This mystery, this blindness, is the dark we must endure, making our way as best we might. It is a darkness so encompassing, so voracious, as to snuff out the sun. Jesus, light of the world, have mercy on us!

Create Us Anew / *Psalm 63*

Stronger than we our sins
a weight as of worlds
rides us under

sterile that burden: wintry
the heart's lucid flow.
Stockstill we stand

hope gone to seed
seed flung to winds.

O be despite all
our winter's end
solace and solstice

Mere shadows we are
lengthening, death-miming

Rumors appall us
the seas are in flood
earth cannot bear our
intolerance, folly.

Forbear. Send a new season
our way, a new will
breaking the shell
of our ill doing.

We rue, would repair.
Create us anew!

St. Ignatius suggests in a meditation on sin, that one consider the very earth rising up against the sinner, threatening to swallow him bodily.

I had thought of this for many years as a kind of holy hyperbole. It was granting the creatures of the earth a kind of extended consciousness that made of them and us an extended family. And wasn't that going too far along the mystical road? What exactly was this practiced man of the world, onetime man of war, lately man of action, getting at?

I had forgotten too much, never truly learned much. Forgotten that tender gaze of Ignatius upon the natural world, where the dumbest and meanest of creatures was eloquent to him. How the stars evoked for him, speechless, the grandeur of God. How he forebore to pluck a flower he admired, so strong was his sense of right ecology, the right relation, the right distance, the rite of non-possession. I had forgotten his tears, the tears of a strong and true believer; in old age he wept so often at the thought of God, they had fears for his very eyesight. The trouble, in sum, being not that he was a mystic, but that I was not. "Earth cannot bear our intolerance, folly."

There are two stages to this folly committed against the earth by us, its rebellious uneasy riders. The first is a kind of shrinking away of the world, a disdain, withdrawal, refusal, before indordinate appetite, cupidity, the sick love of possessions. This, it seems to me, is an act of dying, of willed dying, almost, rather than be violated, debased, put to misuse. No more of that, the gesture says. In one sense, humankind has won; if win it had in mind. But it was a wrong mind from the start; there should have been no question of win (or lose). . . . The earth, its resources, its living creatures, its pure capacity for self-cleansing, self-renewal—this earth was seen as a kind of savage tribe at the edge of consciousness, the edge of the clearing. It must be enslaved or exterminated or both. But in no case could there be intermarriage, or friendship even, with the earth and its creatures. They were for pelts, hides, hooves, teeth; for sport, for killing, for eating, for wasting, for the vicious fun of it; for oil, for perfume, for plumes, for fabrics, for high fashion. The appetite grew as the clearing extended, as the savage earth and its wild beings receded before the guns and the gunmen—civilization.

There could be of course no sense of the mystical in all this. A mystic on the frontier, a mystic in the slave trade, a mystic in the whaling fleet, among trappers, hunters, gold rushers? Improbable.

So we destroyed not only the earth, but the best part of ourselves. Among so predatory a people, who was left to us to weep for the grandeur of the earth? Who would refuse, out of a heightened and precise sense of the rightness of things, so much as to pluck a flower? And what prophet was left to thunder: the earth is rising like an exterminating angel, to destroy its tormentors.

No such voices. Or, if they spoke, they were considered witches, possessed, demonic. (It was we who were demonic.) They were dealt with summarily, brutally, for they interrupted the free flow of death; they presumed to mediate between ourselves and mere things: hides, hooves, pelts, meat, blubber, injuns, niggers, slaves . . . as though such "things" had anything to say to us, the lords of creation, the chosen.

So the tribal creation declined, receded, died out. (Our appetites did not die out.) We did not know it until very late. But when the right order was repeatedly violated, when this or that creature declined toward extinction, something happened to our bodies. We were hacking at ourselves, limbs, organs, piecemeal. We were mutilating our own souls. We were cutting away like mad surgeons, at compassion, justice, fealty, at-homeness, inward peace, discipline, mutuality, modesty. We were blinding the inner eye that saw the crime being committed. We cut out the tongue that would have cried alarm. Few there were left to weep, few to tell of the grandeur of God, few to refuse to pluck a flower, to hunt, to whale, to wage war, to lie and cheat and huckster.

That is the first stage. It is all but over.

The second is rapidly approaching. It all comes together: unbridled technological appetite, resentment against the failing earth, prehuman dread of human variety, malice of the powerless and powerful alike.

It all comes together; the ingredients of the Bomb. Our cry must continue. And our courage. A few must be found to vindicate the outraged tribal earth, the dishonored creator. Lord, send us mystics with hands.

And Where in the World Are You? / *Psalm 73*

I see the wicked glide by
sleek in their velvet hearses
rich beyond measure, egos
puffed like an adder's

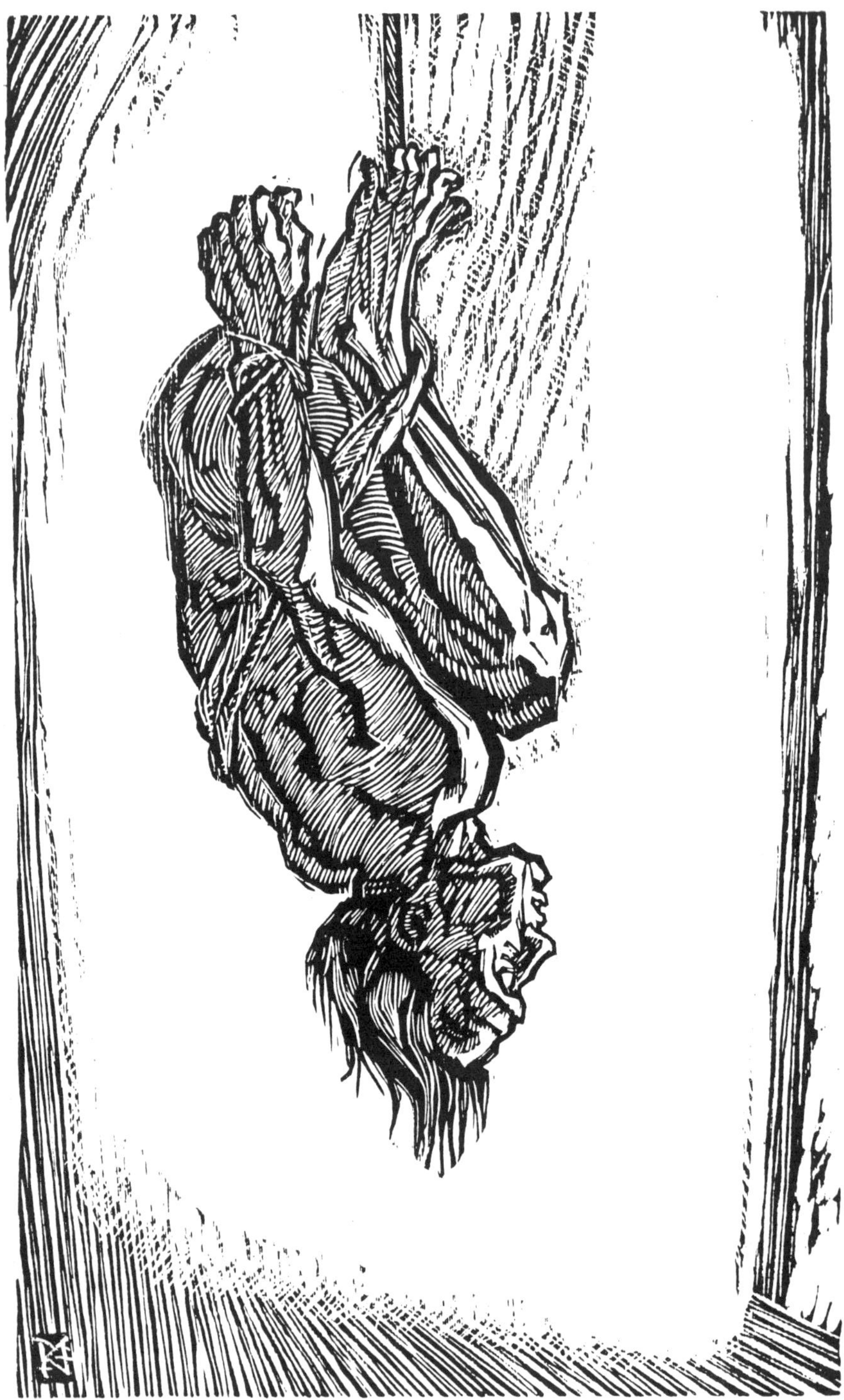

No sons of misfortune these:
no cares
shadow the perfumed brows;
a whirligig of furies
their axletree cuts;
the innocent die.

I sweat like a beast
for the fate of my people.
Is God
ignorant, blank eyed
deaf, far distant
bought off, grown old?

They rape the fair world
they butcher, huckster
by the pound, living flesh;
their guns, their gimlets
claim us for trophy.

Why then endure
why thirst for justice?
Your kingdom-come
a mirage, never comes.

I sweat like a beast
my nightmare is life long
And where in the world
are you?

"Not enough world for need and greed." An old saying of Peter Maurin newly verified, as indeed the world proves not big enough, not rich enough, to bear the burden of bodily hunger and cupidity of spirit.

We had always thought there was enough: water enough, air and land enough, minerals enough, food enough, America enough, world enough.

Or at least those in possession thought so; for the others,

of course, the question did not really signify anything. The earth was ours; for them, was not heaven enough?

Faith Is A Two-Way Street, Hope Is A Hand To Hand Clasp
Psalm 74

Why O God are you silent
why does evil have the upper hand?

The sweet earth is wasted, why?
Torturers crush the bones of the strong
Blank-eyed juntas sit in judgment
Firing squads dispose in a moment's bark
    a single snarl, of the troublesome heroes

Meantime you hide out
meantime you are silent

Maker, ruler of all, into what hands have
        the reins slipped?
The horseman named death
the horseman named plague
the horseman named war
the horseman named hell

They race like mad dogs to the four corners of the world
they round up like an Auschwitz herd, your
    helpless ones

Are you a mere onlooker
        a witness fleeing the murder scene
    one whose evidence, if given, would convict Cain

vindicate the blood of his brother, balance off
the scales in the hand of the blind woman
who for aeons behind her stone bandage
must be thanking her stars for being
blind blind blind

Don't call it contemplation. We need someone other
    than a platonic walker of the sea of tranquility
You, those who speak for you
    taught us to despise
    the otherwordly Others
    eyeballs riveted on the empyrean
    hands innocent of compassion
    white robes, harps, the paraphernalia of parasites

And don't please plead innocence–
            the prophets in your chronicle
    hammer out
scenes of judgment, bring us hangdog
before the court, rake us
with brimstone.

Question arises: whose side are you on?
You weren't always so distant—
Not a page of that famous book doesn't say it.
You—plucking the people from disaster
interposing yourself
turning natural forces around
making sure
making sense
making love
        nailing things down, clarifying,
            repairing, night watching
not allowing evil a rat hole to slink out of

You're clumsy, futile sometimes, fretful,
paternal, a fussy godfather—
At least you're there. Someone to argue with
    push against, yell goddam at,

a public defender, a bondsman
someone to advance a loan
in a lean month
some unexpected courtesy
helping a bad day go down
like a single rose, the luxury
that now and then
is absolute necessity.

Now admit it
everything's fallen apart.
You're nowhere to be found
the roof's down, the place gutted
the rats run the building

You know how their game is played—

  [I don't blame you for it, I can almost see

  the faraway look
  the way you drift off your own page
leaving it blank,
a first page we've got to write
all over again, "in the beginning. . ."]

—It's called Rodent Logic; or, Since The Worst
  Is Inevitable, Let's Help It Along
  With An Electric Shock To The Pants—

THE RODENT THESIS:
Since
the owner of this building can't be found
[if found, could be prosecuted]
let's clean the mess up, just enough
to bring the tenants back
grateful to the new management

THEN
one sweet night when they're abed, attentively counting
papa sheep mama sheep baby sheep

We'll push the button
we'll blast them to powder
we'll send them sky-high
a jig-saw jumble for the nimble fingers
of Genesis One to reassemble

So be it.

In any case,
You're not about to change your habits
Those well-paced aeons of non-intervention
will go on and on. Your own son
couldn't break that shield of silence
He hung his head and died
after such a cry
would have brought a starving bitch from her hole
to comfort a dying whelp

If you must do what you do
if you refuse to do what you could do
If we're to drag on
as best we might, a sorry game

if the youth in a harness of wings
must fall from the sky
the old woman bleed on the pavement
the banks call the shots on the poor
the hooker shiver in the night air
her cute ass bringing in no cash

if this mess, this maelstrom
this funky off-off-off-B'way
badly conceived badly written
badly choreographed
hardly critically acclaimed
[soon to close] show—

Must go on, one more performance
the author-producer-director's
ego inextricably involved

[He's let it be known
through subalterns, press reps
like an invisible billionaire—
"the show's dammit a good one, it'll pick up
he's willing to stake the whole pile on this one."]

It seems arbitrary as that.
The show goes on because you want it to go on.
The show goes on the way you want it to go on.
minor adjustments of time and place
iron necessities skillfully masked—

there's space in the prison scene
for a prison yard
within which inmates
play like mad
at twenty or thirty variations
of a game called FREEDOM.

Doubtless I run a risk
in speaking this way
I sound unregenerate at times, to myself
("the poseur will now mime rebellion")
Yet
innocent blood should have a voice

otherwise butchers become gods
and you take up a butcher's trade

Whatever is outrageous then, ill advised
bitter of tone, heedless, crude in my argument—
forgive
a son does not mince words
compose his agony into "speeches before the court."
out with it
take it or leave it, he's your son

Who you are
is far less clear

given the evidence
daily shoved in our faces—

Let me then make bold to remind you
faith is a two-way street
hope is a hand to hand clasp

so
come believe in me
take my hand

As for that well-known
"our Father who art. . ."
I'll unclench my fist
bloodied at your wall
shake the tears from my face
(that never failing rainfall)
put myself
like a yoga, all will and darkness
in formal stasis, attitude of prayer
will, believe me
keep trying, keep trying, keep trying

The problem of evil is so overwhelming that it threatens to devour us. It does in fact devour many. It is their master enigma, so to speak, the clue to non-understanding, despair, the darkness covering the face of the earth.

Because evil is the only problem, no God can possibly exist. As the problem is commonly stated, it seems to me that such a conclusion is inevitable. Evil overwhelms us because we stand within the so-called problem, up to our necks, like the guilty in Dante's inferno. We miss our plight precisely because it is our own, not a "problem" at all, not "out there," in a malfunctioning universe, but here, now, under this skin, in this skull, wrought by these choices. We are good consumers, even while we question "the system" which feeds our appetites like captive animals, on the hour. We are a people who prepare doomsday weapons, pay for them, are silent about their existence—even as we purportedly seek peace. We are intelligent serpents, our own tails are our menu.

One could suggest another tack than the merely problematic, which seems to me to get nowhere. The original sin of Genesis, with its murderous overtones, offers a clue. Murder breaks out, the slaying of one brother by another. And in time (not much time was required) murder was legitimated; it became a quite ordinary event. Weaponry was taken in hand again and again as a way of resolving human conflict. Get rid of one (or both) of the parties, and you get rid of the difficulty. Could anything be neater, swifter? Cain was the ancester, Hitler the natural descendant. Not to speak of the nuclear Strangeloves.

In such a way the original sin remains original, in the sense that murder can always be resorted to, new weaponry dreamed up, the old quarrels renewed, when all else (as they love to say) has been tried and has failed. (Which is to say, in the ordinary course of power diplomacy, when practically nothing has been tried; when that little has quite predictably failed.) So murder is invoked, incanted even, consecrated (the appeal to religion, the response of religion, is mandatory); the scope of murder is enlarged (each war must be bigger to make its point; the percentage of civilian deaths must increase to make a point); the murder must be immaculately justified (hence the requirement of an ever more stringent ideology of Our Superior Moral Rectitude). It must also be technologized (the making of our point requires us to multiply indiscriminately the capacity of weaponry; bomb them back to the Stone Age).

In such ways, murder becomes the ordinary menu of ordinary folk in the twentieth century. The motto: you are what you eat. Now if you, dear reader, dear Christian (or I), catch your breath now and again with a gasp of pure horror, if you are wrenched about by a demon hand with the thought—what are they doing to us and to our children, what are they doing to the children of the world?—such episodes after all mean nothing except a tic of memory, a recidivist spasm so to speak, the vagrant phantasm of a hypersensitive conscience, long ignored, long pacified, almost extinct. Still, here and there, in out-of-the-way religious gatherings, in corners and cellars, even in churches, people still gather and dare to ask questions which the times themselves have declared, if not absurd, then beyond answering. Like: can there not be another way? Can no one show it to us? Who will lead us to a human future? And if we push away in disgust from the cannibal feast, how are we to survive?

The part so-called religion has played in inflaming and justifying violence is part of the tragedy of history. The tragedy has had a long run; it is still playing. Have no fear dear Christians, God is with us, our country right or wrong. Thus a blessing is invoked on the hideous banquet of war, the guests lean forward in silence; with gusto, with a good conscience, they tie their napkins about, balance knife and fork, await the entree.

But faith is more tentative, shows more pain and less certainty. A faithful few refuse the menu and are, of course, punished for bad manners. Not at all certain about "sides: God on ours." Not possessing Him, not having the key to His conduct. Sensing obscurely indeed, that such keys are usually in the hands of the mighty, the guardians of good fortune, the keepers of prisons, the nuclear jugglers. Please note, too, the scene, the geography of faith. The faithful do not hang around the banquet, tempted here, nibbling there, hoping to reform the institution of eating humans. Not trying to formulate Nine or Ten Conditions for a Just Cannibalism. The banquet is not a good scene, such folk say stubbornly; they are intolerable spoilers, beyond converting. They keep saying things like, the banquet cannot really be reformed.

The plain trouble is, human beings are the main course. And they shouldn't be. This is not a very exalted morality. We're not particularly proud of it. We ought to be able in such an advanced century to go further than that. But there you are, we're stuck with saying no to a question that should never have arisen in the first place: whether human beings ought to eat human beings. What a question!

They go further; they insist the question can't even be discussed in the banquet hall. It's too late, it's the wrong place. For as a matter of fact, the menu is already agreed on; somewhere in the vast kitchens, victims are already being brought in. You can read it in the eyes of the guests; they've paid for such and such a meal, they've worked hard for a night out, they're not about to sit there and put up with a change of menu, substitutions. Have you ever seen Americans, those who know the good smell and feel of money, who know how it speaks loud and moves fast and gets things done? Have you ever seen such people take the ruination of a big evening lying down? Cut off their supply, say the faithful few. Tell the truth where it's never been told, where the truth is forbidden, open the question in IRS offices, courtrooms, prisons, Pentagon (a few years ago, draft file centers); this is where we speak from, where we act from. . . .

You know how this sort of thing ends. The other name of faith, its wordly name, its baptismal name, is trouble. The faithful are in trouble: all the rest are dreaming of that feast, saving toward it, counting on it. Thus the problem of evil, the problem of a cannibal culture.

The feast is by now a national observance.

It requires the following: skill, nerve, persistence, corrupt religion, big appetites, profit motives, main speakers, cleanup crews, military hard and software, taxes and taxpayers, voters, the chefs (chiefs of staff), a military band, beautiful voracious women, heroes in battle dress, thirty-five gun salutes, a chief in whose honor "Hail to the Chief" may be struck up. And then, of course, since the banquet is international in flavor and principle, all sorts of foreign lackeys, subalterns, colonels, shahs, and *their* retinue and network of torturers, hit men, police, soldiers, et cetera et cetera.

In any case, no light on the human predicament.

In any case, darkness upon darkness. . . .

The prophets speak of another way.

A crisis, an outcry, a burning question.

They have no seat at the banquet, their world is an outer darkness. There, for all their clumsy, abrupt speech, stubborn silence, refusals to negotiate, they have won the right to question God. For they have renounced the bloody meat, the infernal feast of history. Their very lives are a question. Not a problem, but an expression of the mystery.

They are the "other side" of the mystery of evil. Which is

to say, they are the mystery of goodness. They speak for life, their lives speak for it. Their lives lead further, beyond themselves. Further, to Jesus, who being innocent of all crime, was slain.

It is not enough, it will never be enough to ask: why are humans evil? A question as futile as: why are humans inhuman?

No, the real question, the question which appalls and puts to silence, the question which is avoided in principle and neglected in fact, the question for which is substituted every trick of technology, every nostrum of psychology, all the airy and groundless ground rules of "religion"—the real question seems to me quite simple. For instance: what is a human being? And how may we become human once more, in a bestial time?

Of one thing we may be fairly certain. Those who sit at the feast, those complicit in crimes against humanity, will never come on the question. They are too busy eating, they have eaten their own souls.

The Lord Appears, The Mighty Scurry For Cover *Psalm 76*

A terror to the great ones
is our God

How they dread him
this breaker of arrows

Armed to the teeth, the warmakers flee like chaff
He wrests their ill-gotten lands, their blood drenched
borders

And the valiant sleep;
spears, swords at side
inert, gunmetal cold

The Lord appears;
chariot, charioteer, they fall
broken like stones

The Lord appears
the mighty
scurry for cover
judgment at hand!

[*The lowly stand firm*
he beckons them to his side]

The Lord appears;
princes, satraps
whimper like infants

A terror to the great of the earth
is our God.

Unfortunately for all sides, in the Bible God is impelled to take sides. Or so it seems. He stands against the warriors, kings, killers, architects of violence, pharaohs, slave masters. And from the first pages, he stands with Abel, Noah, Abraham (but also Isaac the near victim), Jacob; and later with David (reservedly), Moses, the exiles, the desert remnant.

In time, his preferences grow reasonably clear, consistent. They grow more than clear in the case of Jesus—blindingly self-evident. This young rabbi claims a privileged place in the line of prophets. He steps calmly into that place and promptly pays for it with his blood. And God, the great Absenter, Abstainer, albeit tardily, is with him; in a stupendous intervention, the dead man walks again.

We have to insist—in a century ridden with division, hatred, distrust—that in so acting, Jesus and God his father

were doing something more profitable to us, more significant, than merely taking sides. (What an abstract notion that is, after all, stale, fraught with jealousy, ego. Can we not offer something better to our times, to the people of the mid-70s, castaways, survivors?)

I think we can. I think we can be confident that in announcing his vocation

> He has sent me to proclaim good news to the poor, release for prisoners, recovery of sight for the blind, to let the broken victims go free. . . .

In this, he is not excluding the jailer, the rich, the high and mighty of this world. Indeed, he stands for all, speaks for all, suffers for all, overleaps death for all. Either this is true, or, it seems to me, he does these things in vain, finally, for no one. For the warlike as for the meek, for the valiant as for the pusillanimous, for the mighty as for the lowly. Finally, for sinners. . . .

In saying this, we are not attempting to make him into a graham cracker for every deadened taste. No, he stands somewhere, he is visible to the moral sense, he speaks aloud, outrages the conventional. If he takes sides, if he excoriates the hypocrites, it is to unwind the infection veiled in swath upon swath of deceit, respectability. He unmasks conflict, he exposes long festering hatreds. It is in this sense that he seems to take sides for the present, for the unfinished, poisoned, broken present, in order that sides need not be taken forever.

Remember "the surgeon with the wounded hands." Remember, "In order to be healed, our sickness must get worse."

As I reflect on these things, a message is sent to me. Five friends have been arrested for pouring their own blood on the river portico of the Pentagon. Others are arrested at the same hour for digging a symbolic grave on the lawn.

A Catholic bishop in Rhodesia is sentenced to ten years for opposing the racist policies of that country.

A Korean bishop is imprisoned for protesting the denial of civil rights to citizens. And so on and so on.

Are these resisters worthy of their tradition? Of the Gospel?

The lowly stand firm
he beckons them to his side

Their lives are offered for the healing of the nations. They are taking sides now, that sides need not be taken forever.

Carry It On, Urges The Lord
Psalm 78

Hear me people, I have tales to tell
parables, mysteries unveiled.

"Carry it on," the Lord urged
"Great deeds, unsurpassed works–
If you forget, bravado and revolt will rule you
No single spirit, no common will–
sunk in the past, base idolaters
just like your fathers before you."

. . . .

First came the breaking of pledges.
Amnesiac, they wander about
like sun-struck lizards.

Yet for their sake he transformed
night into day, rude seas into footpaths–

No matter. Dim wits, blind eyes.
They put God to the test. "Here in the desert

He'll scrounge us a meal?" They mocked Him
after the struck rock, shouting torrent.

A banquet cloth, a snowfall of manna
a cloud of bread,   the migrants
ate, drank from his hand.

. . . .

South wind, west wind, a rain of blessing–
he traced a line in the sea, dry-shod they passed over
A guiding hand by day, a starry night passage—

But love of possessions seduced them
They fashioned a bestial figure, bowed to it
hell's sycophants. Broke the covenant
like dry sticks. Tried, provoked him
like a baited beast. He stood there
patient as Job.

Stood there, endured there. Tried this, dared that.
Flails, furies, plagues–
pollution came down
their waters stank
the heavens lowered, a millstone
earth rolled up

a magician's carpet

Came hailstorm and brimstone   locusts and foul frogs
oceans befouled,   oil spills and swill

Came blood to the cup and snakes to the bridal and maggots
to fruit trees and stench to the skies
Hailstones ripped the vines
ice split the sycamores
rot on the cattles' hooves
fevers' breath on the flocks

Distress, unease of spirit
No visions in youth, no dreams in old age

Remorse in the guts, dread of life
anxiety, hatred unbounded
Distrust, venality, death

. . . .

No deliverance.

Ersatz saviors, tumbling like clowns
Out of rabbit holes, top hats, paper hoops–

abracadabra   hocus pocus   open sesame

salvation   maudition   lambastian

follow me   swallow me

. . . .

And a curse laid on the first-born

Brazen they withstood Him face to face.
Hardened, edgy, chips of the old block.

They bowed to their trumpery
idols, their crime beyond crime.
"We have other gods. Begone."

Tainted seed,   arrows
tipped with venom, devious, faithless
idol makers,   breakers of covenant.

. . . .

He gave up, turned his back
left his tent empty

And youths withered like grass
and maids mourned at the altar,
no priest at the sacred fire
no widows' lament.

. . . .

Then
He shook the sleep from his eyes
like a warrior brain fuddled with wine.

Lonely He went, seeking David, His chosen one.
Found him in mid-pasture, amid flocks
ewes heavy with offspring.

The friends embraced;
"come feed my sheep, feed my lambs."

and he does so with all his heart, to this day.

Teachableness: a long word and clumsy, and I apologize for it. Still, I cannot find a better, to express one of the noblest qualities I know of.

To me it speaks of a right sense of things, self-measure taken, one's place rightfully judged—not in a blind box of privilege, but under a big sky; one's place in a grand order of being. A teachable person; creaturely before a mystery that summons, reproves, sets limits, blesses, urges forward, illumines. Yes, and crushes, kills, resurrects. The opposite of teachableness I take to be a kind of "playing God," a capricious role, prideful, at odds with reality, a kind of derring-do, essentially alienating and destructive. When seriously undertaken, its outcome is murder.

The opposite of playing God is certainly not playing human. All appearances, all attempts to the contrary notwithstanding. Indeed, it seems as though the modern world were a continuous spectacle of this kind, a parade of mannikins on display, under the cruel glare, the big blare—in sports, politics, professions, entertainment—for the most part, offering not much more than a spiffy stereotype. They go with the prevailing winds, sycophants, cultists of money and skin, silent before political tyranny, consecrated competitors. They subordinate service to the care and feeding of idols (security, ego, dolce vita). Such people, for all their panache, are only playing human. Mask, costume, style, is the message. In the face of our desperate hunger for truth, for guiding spirits, for courage and integrity, their message is strictly bad news.

Then what is the good news? The opposite of a clumsy lie is not a skillful lie. That way lie death, deception, power politics, the bear pit of public woe. The opposite of all this immemorial and bloody nonsense is truthfulness, rebirth, teachableness, the refusal to "play" anything, the courage to be.

The bitter adventure narrated in psalm 78, I suggest, is being played out with devastating exactness today, in America. Please ponder the poem in this light, sensibly, with an eye to our time and place, attuned to our own (perhaps mortal) illness, our willful fooling with limitless sex, flagrant weaponry, the green paper chase. Thus regarded, as a searching light on our own predicament, the psalm may reach our hearts, render them less stony, less impervious to the truth. . . .

The image that closes the psalm seems to me surprising, surgically exact, a stroke of truth. God is like a sleeper, like one awakened from a stupor of wine. Everything before (even to Him) has been a kind of pre-thought, a fog of wrong starts, appearances, mirages, effort gone awry, complexity, paternalism. Now He shrugs it all off—a bad dream; He comes to a better mood. He wanders out of the house into the fields, lonely, seeking a friend. And He finds one. A phase is over, not only for the people, but for God. He is no longer playing God. He is no longer "playing" anyone. He has come through the messy labyrinth of superintending the universe. Let it come, let it go. At length, let me be myself. What I was seeking all along, and did not know it, was a friend.

Must not God too be teachable? How beautiful, how daring a thought. And especially the further implication, that the end of teaching is simply wisdom. A wisdom that is conferred when all defenses, armaments, rhetoric and roles, self-importance, bumptiousness are dropped, let go. The great and lovely and life-infusing equalizer is—love. Amen.

Lord Of Life Have Mercy On Us
Psalm 82

Our Lord is God
his judgment is near, is at hand!

the big wigs and small
the down & out the up & coming
the boisterous the preposterous
the left fielders the right wingers
doves hawks eagle scouts
the motley and mortified
flag wavers free loaders

What a procession!

it halts, it falls like a wind-threshed field.
the scythe ranging wide and far
(those bony implacable arms
those harvester's hands!)

—like the newborn fawn's
legs sheared off in the long grass

eyes half open in birth
half closed in death

harvest and planting
(the hunter
stuffs his sack and strides on—)

Lord of death
lord of life
have mercy on us!

ALL ALL COME BEFORE YOU
BIG WIGS AND SMALL
THE DOWN & OUT
THE UP & COMING
THE BOISTEROUS THE PREPOSTEROUS
LEFT FIELDERS RIGHT WINGERS
THE MOTLEY THE MORTIFIED
FLAG WAVERS FREE LOADERS

WHAT A PROCESSION!

EVERY ONE CUT DOWN
THE SCYTHE RANGING WIDE AND FAR
(THOSE BONY IMPLACABLE ARMS
THOSE HARVESTER'S HANDS!)

LIKE THE NEWBORN FAWN'S
LEGS SHEARED OFF IN THE LONG GRASS

BUNDLED IN
GUTS AND SPRING WHEAT
EYES
HALF OPENED IN BIRTH
HALF CLOSED
IN DEATH

HARVEST AND PLANTING
THE HUNTER
STUFFS HIS SACK AND STRIDES ON

HAVE MERCY ON US
HAVE MERCY

PSALM 81

So much wrong in the world, every infant rocking in an uneasy cradle, people dying with that look on their faces, of roads taken that turned into cul de sacs—who could presume to set it all right? Are we born lefthanded into a righthanded world? Are we simply born into the wrong world? Will someone tell us please? Will God tell us?

But you see (so it's said) He's part of the wrong. Didn't He set it all in motion in the first place? By His own claim? Moreover, didn't He, on occasions too numerous to mention, refuse to come to the rescue—even for the sake of His own son?

Doesn't the world, all said, go its own sweet way, as if indeed He didn't exist at all?

What therefore makes this "hypothesis" called God necessary at all? There is of course, no satisfactory answer to this difficulty. So much of its force depends, as is said these days, on "where you're coming from." So many suppositions, so much invisible writing, so much taken for granted. . . .

Almost anyone, given the fraternal, sororal, egalitarian temper of life, is undoubtedly capable of concocting a better god than the one who is said to exist. Almost anyone plucked from the street knows more than He, is wiser, has a surer sense of the way things should go, knows the way the wind blows, is more logical, more skilled in the arts, whether martial, amatory or literary. Almost anyone could write a more sensible Bible than the author-in-residence.

All this is of course predictable; possibly it is even a kind of backhanded compliment. It would be a poor excuse of a god after all, who couldn't create his own successor; a poor stick of a father whose son couldn't (at least on paper) improve on the old man.

A poor American, finally, who couldn't play an old religio-cultural game, already two centuries old, part of his inheritance so to speak. And consisting, in essence, of two well tested steps, stages, principles. To wit:

——When things are going well (i.e., in accord with your claims, whether of ego, ethical or ethnic superiority, or simple frontier homespun savvy, assign as initiating cause and guiding genius of this perfectly normal state of affairs—ourselves! Which is to say, translate that iridescent energetic reality, our way of life, into its nuts and bolts: our gross national product, our motherhood, our free enterprise, etc., etc.

——When things go ill (i.e., when we run up against competing ideologies, voracious third world appetites, Vietnams), at that point begin to question the faulty judgment, poor timing, lack of discernment of—God. In the first case (above) He may rightly be regarded as an appendage of our righteousness, a welcome arrangement in the secular temple. In the second, a dark, even tragic element enters; since He is supposed to be on our side, in accord with our just desserts and his holy will—then why isn't He?

One can only note that the stated principles, in light of psalm 82, are, to say the least, questionable. In two regards:

——The American translation of *well* and *ill* differs radically from that of Jesus and the prophets.

——A dialogue with God, inevitably tragic in character, is never carried on from the catbird seat. The book of Job is insistent on this point, as is the book of Jesus. Evidently, that seat is occupied already, by a character drawn from American fiction—*The Devil and Daniel Webster.* The occupant is not D. Webster.

Turn Turn Turn / *Psalm 85*

I hear your voice
turn turn turn;
peace to your friends
to the faithful few.

The earth yields its harvest
the Lord's goodness breaks forth.
Praise him!
He turns to us, we
return to Him.

Another of those lovely little outbursts of the poet. It seems no more than a plume of smoke on the horizon. But what a fire it gives notice of!

Our fate is irretrievably bound up with that of the world we dwell in. This is a very old and common truth; the kind we used to stuff away in attics and cellars, the kind that was trotted out, we fondly thought, only by old wives and their old consorts. Now we know it, with the bitter knowledge that is of questionable use because it arrives so late; the knowledge is out of the closet, out of the attic, it walks about like an arrogant skeleton.

It came so late. We had heard before in our history of the breakup of this or that "way of life." We had seen the scourge of war upraised in our lifetime; indeed, we had wielded that scourge mercilessly. Pogroms, tiger cages, torture, a holocaust (several holocausts), refugees, prisoners shuttled about between "sides" like tons of convertible waste, the breakup of heart, mind, public structure, law, order, compassion, church, school—in fact, we had seen just about everything go. At least, we supposed, in all this muck and chaos the ground is still firm beneath our feet. Such things have happened before, people have always rebuilt, started over. There was always earth enough. . . . But there is no longer earth enough.

There are two forces gathering (or rather, already gathered), to bring this unimaginable thing to pass. Not one force, but two. One speedy, the other slower, more methodical, but proceeding apace; and "slower" only in a most relative way. From another point of view, it proceeds at breakneck speed. But the first is a bolt of lightning. The first is that concentration, that distilling of the energy of the earth. When this energy was dissipated in the earth, it was part of its diurnal vein, the richness, the volatile energy. But Mephistopheles instructed his pupil long and well; they labored for secret years and together they wrung the earth of its secret. Their product is now a baleful essence; labeled anti-earth. Wrenched from the heart of the world, it boils away in cauldrons, it is loaned out, traded to other nations; like a yeast starter, it can be indefinitely renewed, energized, added to, heated up. It has destroyed two cities. And it can end the world.

The other anti-earth force is that of the great Dollar. It is a sign of power so awesome as to remind one of the mark of Cain, multiplied a thousandfold on the foreheads of men and women. It is their tribute to the Dollar-god, whose sign is his own serpentine body twisted about a stake. What promises he makes to his devotees, what punishment he inflicts on nonbelievers!

He too can bring down the earth—by eating it alive. He is not the warmaker Mars, the Great Boom. He is rather the Endless Eater. In his corporate head, plans are concocted for the seizure, crushing and ingesting of the earth; in this he is a python. But in his tooth is the poison that deranges, paralyzes, puts to death.

The Endless Eater is in truth a cannibal. He eats the earth, he eats people. That is why he is brother to the Bomb.

"Adore me" is his cry, as it is the cry of the Bomb.

We may take our choice. In reality it makes little difference; to adore one is to serve the other, and vice versa. They have a pact, one will never evangelize among the other's faithful, nor trample his sanctuary. Common cause, so to speak; interlocking interests.

As for ourselves, our choices are not large. According to these Awesome Estimables, we have only the one or the other, to name our god, submit to, to become true believers of.

But to persons of faith, the situation is other; these two appear in a different guise; neither awesome nor estimable. But contemptible, stereotyped, void. New masks on the old, old artful dodger—death.

That is why the psalm is both delicious and apt. It summons us; it sings in its lovely old fashioned Shaker way. Turn, turn, turn. Turn in another direction, that of True God. If the choices are few, it is better perhaps to die with one's face turned toward the truth, than to sell one's soul to the armpit of death. Not entirely satisfactory perhaps; but on the whole, a better turn.

Still I Would Be Your Faithful Servant / *Psalm 88*

I hear
only
the closing of doors
the turning of locks.
Friends
(friends?)
freeze at sight of me.
Is this your doing?
   misfortune my middle name?

They pass by, heads airborne
   supernal or worldly business—
priests, pariahs, making it big
passing the buck, concocting
pie in the sky.

      Day and night I cry out to you
      No other, no help for me.
      Come then, samaritan—

Out of sight, out of mind
I wander this no man's land

The living
wash hands of me
the dead
close eyes against me
Worse;
You
turn away.

The thought of death crosses me—
cold comfort.
What comfort to you
my death
that cold shoulder
that icy touch—

In hell who praises you?
who magnifies your deeds?
hell's chorus
spontaneous, breathless
striking up
Alleluia Alleluia?

Still I would be
[misfortunate, maladroit]
your faithful servant

Yet
day after day
your blows rain down

You winnow my friends
they vanish like chaff
you leave me
for only
familiar—

night

A prayer like this one is not often heard these days. Shame? Fear? We're caught in a dilemma—the psalmist seems to despair, yet he prays, he prays out his despair.

We have things all mixed up. How can despair turn to God? How can God attend to despair?

The trouble is our own; neither God's, nor the psalmist's. The trouble is the narrow range of emotion, need, prescience, devotion, yearning, which is allowed to come for-

ward at prayer; like a row of scrub-faced children, Sunday speeches tripping from their tongues. God sits there like an aging superintendant, bored but benign, takes it all in, nods sagely, applauds. It is all perfectly harmless and everyone knows it. Nothing will come of it, everyone knows it. Sunday school will go on as it was. The world will go on as it was.

The idea would be laughable were it not so sorrowful.

We open the bible, we seek out Jesus. A shocking life passes by. We cannot grasp it, take it in. An explosion of energy, an implosion of stillness. The impossible is continually surmounted, pushed back and back. Where only outer darkness seemed in command, he stands; suddenly the human has won another space to occupy, to be itself in.

Then it comes home to us, what penny whistlers we are in the world's graveyard. Afraid, and afraid to admit it. Or forbidden our fear, cleaned up, put on stage for religious "exercises" that test nothing except our infinite capacity for boredom. The range of our lives constantly narrowing, the range of acceptable conduct. We dress for a party exactly as we are dressed in death. The third option or event (and the same costume) being Sunday churchgoing. Alas for us, we die before we fairly live. The acceptable clothing seems to me an apt symbol for the acceptable emotion, the acceptable religious stance. In the Great Sunday School in the sky, if I am to win a hearing (so the theory goes, enforced in a hundred subtle ways) I must appear as one whose life is roundly successful, in a world that makes sense (making sense being roughly equivalent to making money) one whom the pain of life never affrights or affronts or bowls over. Indifferent, morally neutral; or if morally opinionated, then well hidden in a herd of look alikes. But never, God save the mark, so impolitic, so uncouth, as to grow passionate.

All sorts of lamentable consequences of this might be pointed out. One thinks of the multitudes who tread the wheel of life like beasts drawing up water from a dry well. We look up, we cry out, it is all the same. The wheel keeps turning, the people trudging. What benefit or blessing there is, the why of it all, possibilities, hints, recourse, cries, responses, the light of freedom, breakthrough—what have these to do with us? Our reasoning, like our bodies, like our impoverished gestures, all move in a closed circle. No breaking out.

One could go on. Creatures like ourselves are whipped into shape (into shapelessness), morally inert, our passion surgically removed like a circumcision, at birth. Shortly thereafter we fall in line. We submit to authority good and bad, we grow fatalistic, we accept the shape of things as inevitable. The shape of life today. How terrible to reflect that Christians, people like ourselves, have been seized on as perfect instruments for fascism, nazism. And, dare we say it, for Americanism?

We allowed the Vietnam war to go on for some fifteen years of multiplied horror. Most of us found our lives not at all thrown off track by the longest, bloodiest crime in all our history. It is as though a Kitty Genovese, with a Vietnamese face, were being slowly with exquisite cruelty, murdered under our window. She cried out for many hours, for days, for years. The murder went on. She was a child, she was a village woman, she knew nothing of ideology, of why she must die, of what passion drove the knife. She knew only that she was dying. She sensed there were humans about, listening at the darkened windows. Where were they? How could they let her die, for years and years?

Alas, it was our eyes that stared out in the darkness (stared at the tube). Only we can answer the question, which is now the question of the dead: where were you, why did you not answer my cries?

We were not passionate, we were not religious, we were incapable even of a saving despair. We were busy about that other business, a business which consumes, which is called business as usual. Which consumes like hellfire. What is the name of that business? Why should it be so imperative? Why may nothing come between it and ourselves, not even the cries of a dying woman?

The business is called—our own dying. It is this infernal decline of our powers, decline of passion, of clairvoyance, of courage, of outreach, of chancetaking; this business must be attended to, at all cost. The argument is beyond argument. We are like a huge corporation of morticians. Death is our business, and business is good. We spend our lives among the dead, preparing corpses for view, setting them up, propping them in windows, applying cosmetics to dead blemishes. In an irony too deep for words, we make a living off the dead. And it is the dead who come to look most like us. The ideal corpse, the ads imply, is the lifelike one. And who do we look like?

And it is the living who pay; the survivors, the grieving; the whole world in fact, which orbits, faster and even closer, around a great embalmed corpse, its own ikon and image. A bomb? No, the Bomb.

We die this way, because we have never lived. Because we have been dying from our birth; because a way of life, self-exalted, specious, death ridden, a con job, a huckster's pitch, forbade us to live, from childhood. Many stories of hopes brought down, of exultant overflowing life sternly punished, banished to darkness—as many stories as there are women and men in the world, almost.

We waste not only our own lives, we waste the world. There may soon be no world left to waste. It is a sober prediction, made by experts, they have repeated it many times. No world for the children; no children.

The prospect, horrid as it is, is greeted by many with a kind of horrid relief; no reaction, no outcry, no resistance. We prefer the day after death to the day before it. A huge sigh of relief, like air from a stabbed lung. So we are dying, make it fast. . . .

Please read the psalm, slowly; give it time. It is one thing to read the words as one would read a weather report, casual news. It is quite another to read as though one's life depended on the truth. Do our lives depend on the truth, or the untruth? God knows we walk in darkness, that we have sown darkness. Let us say it, dwell on it, let it penetrate us; stand still there in the dark, knowing we can go no further, petrified with dread. There seems no where to go.

The psalm denies this, the great denial.

There is somewhere to go. But no one comes on the way, who remains pure American. For them, Kitty Genovese may die and be damned.

If this were so, if God were as petrified, cold blooded as we, if our stagnation were acceptable, a religion even—then why bother? We were better off dead—which is to say, exactly where we are.

But where might we be, if we believed, if we dared hope?

You / *Psalm 90*

Before ever the mountains arose
[blind from birth they were, mute, dumb]
You. Are.

Before the seas
before the first dawn
You.

From dust to dust the human story
a crooked line, quickly effaced

You endure
You summon
Come; mere sunstruck motes
[Adam stands there, Eve radiant there]

then
their course run—
again
"Come"

They wither like grass, the perfect and proud.
Words die, suns set, grass blows, a dust.

What then?
we must learn
time and again
like infants, on hands and knees
spasmodic wisdom. Six months, sixty years

all one
one blind tug,
at the empyrean. Teach us to count our days
multiple, scanty, no matter. But a voice of praise.

One approaches middle age with a sense of hair raising astonishment. Where did the years go? What have they accomplished? I hold a hand before my eyes. How the veins stand out! And that look that looks back at me from the mirror—truculent? Bewildered? Wise at last? Perhaps an uneasy mix of all of these. But still . . . that face; is one not responsible for it? Is it not at last (God help me) one's own? It is. The thought is at considerable distance from comfort. Closer to what the poet called "carrion comfort."

It is not so much folly, dread, fear, or, on the other hand, triumph, pride in accomplishment, that the psalmist evokes. Everyone takes his chance on such things; we see highly differing visions in the mirror, mirror on the wall.

But what strikes so fierce a blow is simply the breakneck speed of it. Where did the years go, once they were gone?

Such a sense of puzzlement occurs at a certain point on the road. At the middle point, inevitably.

A stage has been reached, an accounting is due. Suddenly a bill is thrust into one's hand. The debtor may be blind, insolvent; it makes no difference; the issue is not you, but the account owed. Pay up!

Or another image. One is suddenly thrust into a large

room filled with people. A formal gathering, all faces turn toward you. Will you say something? Expectation widens their eyes, silences all tongues. Say what? You are struck dumb, terrified. And the faces turn away in scorn. At the end, I think, when all the worry and bickering are done with, you leave such nightmares (such realities?) to another.

So the speeches are forgotten, the bills unpaid. But how could such images evoke one's life at all, life in God, life with others—how carry their weight, their complexity, their hot and cold rhythms? They were not images of reality at all, but phantom nightmares.

What is it the saint wrote? "In the evening, we will be judged by love."

Rescuer, Consoler, Friend
Psalm 94

Happy the one you raise up Lord
to esteem your law
evil days will not touch him

But the wicked—
their thoughts are a mockery; this God
sees nothing, hears nothing, says nothing!

They carry their heads high
They weave cunning words. To hear them talk
oppression, war mongering
greed, duplicity, were noble endeavors!

They hold kangaroo courts, the just
they condemn out of hand

Law And Order! they cry
lawlessness, disorder are all their skill.

God of strict requital, judge them!
Lest they prevail forever
mockers, mimics of justice
torturers, liars
piling their booty sky-high
on the bowed backs of the poor . . .

There is one who speaks for me
There is one who judges in justice
When an evil snare all but trips me
He is there, rescuer, consoler, friend

He will utterly destroy them
(they utterly destroy themselves)
To me, he has shown another face—
rescuer, consoler, friend.

What faith shines through these prayers! And at the same time, what clearsighted understanding of the workings of this world. We would like to be able to separate the two.

Faith without experience of the world is easily dismissed as naiveté, childishness. That is how primitives go about, or children, we say. Then on the other hand, worldly experience without faith. The condition of most of us, at least to a degree. It justifies our cynicism; there is no taste of God in our mouth, only the ashes of this world.

I think the claim to worldly wisdom ought to be challenged, where it asserts itself as having no need of faith. What kind of wisdom is that? We ought to ask our own soul. We ought to put the question to others, ought not imply by silence that this is a great thing, honorable, worthy of close attention. Or even, as often occurs, imply that faithful people (among whom we take our half-hearted stand) are less hip, less "relevant."

If we ourselves had faith, if we approached the worldly (understood as those in possession of this world, but derelict of God), we would know what such "wisdom" is—to the core. It is because we ourselves come to life as neutrals, heads a little to one side with bemusement, curious in a mild sort of way, infected with myths of equality and tolerance; for this reason we offer no edge, no fire, no music.

The psalmist does. He is not interested in buts or rebuttals, he is interested in the truth. He does not debate with an adversary, he takes account of his world, including his adversaries, and he offers a prayer—a prayer which gives us a glimpse into his soul (as they say today, his soul-in-the-world), a phenomenon charged with secret fires, where others might, if they wish, light their lamps.

That acute sense of right and wrong! We would blunt it, the instrument turns against our own sweet flesh, in the wrong as we are often. (But secretly in the wrong, known only to ourselves, the blade safely sheathed, and we unwounded.) But the psalmist is constantly whetting his edge, he wants a line drawn clear, even if it must be drawn in his own flesh. (But precisely there is the rub—or, rather, the pain of entry. In his case not welcomed, but withstood. In our case, sweated over a thousand times in anticipation, until the pain of truth becomes a nightmare more terrifying than death.)

The psalmist calls the world as he sees it, the outlines are jagged, sharp; it is high noon in his mind, no blur, no fog. In salons, in churches, in universities, in courts of law, they would shake their heads, call him extremist; you must modify your language, you cannot win good folk to "your cause" that way. (Love that *your;* it is always your war must be opposed, not mine; your injustice not mine, and so on. My conscience is your caboose; puff on.)

In the psalms we have a saving embarrassment; which is to say, God is involved in the language, the judgment, the sensibility. Such a statement is sufficient to throw a liberal poll into a panic. One is tempted to parapharse John's Gospel. "If we say the psalms are of God, people will say, why do you not believe? If we say they are not, the people will stone us. . . ." It is a dilemma more delicious than morning dew. God an extremist?

Also worth noting, from a tactical point of view, our friend of the poem has not resorted to abuse, yells, or stoning his adversaries. How he deals with them in the world, we do not know. But we know that on occasion of their crimes against him and others, he does a simple thing—he turns to God in prayer. An example worthy of note. And of inference. If he thus invokes God as his third party, advocate, friend, patron, brother; is not this turning away from hatred, recrimination, even an intemperate demand for justice—is not this a clue to his conduct in the fray? One thinks so.

There is another point. When faith is in question, geography is everything. Where one stands, I mean to say. It is quite imaginable, for example, that the adversaries of the psalmist also turn to God. All sorts and conditions of people do; from the saints, through you and me, to Hitler, as we are told. We have no notion of the wording of Hitler's prayer; one shudders at the thought of reconstructing it. We do know that our own prayer at times, is infected with delusions, whether of grandeur or of nitpicking. More, we have examples of prayers throughout history that were variously otiose, bloodthirsty, childish, anti-Semitic, racist, governed by all the witless fancies of the heated brain. Prayers made with the expectation, not that God will plunge in the flames, refashion the grotesque inhuman heart—but that He will bend His will to the worshipper's way, that He will bless folly and crime and blindness. That is the horror.

In any case, God too has a geography. He stands somewhere. Where that is, the psalm gives more than a hint. In this poem and others, it is clear that He stands, and stands and stands, in one and the same place: at the side of the just, in the midst of trouble, facing the adversaries. And that would seem to be the point of this prayer, and of any prayer for help in distress. Not that God must be drawn by threads or cables out of His empyrean neutrality; but that He is near, at hand, at all times, but most pressingly (one almost said breathingly) when justice is assailed, and the life or death of the innocent is in question.

Prayer thus heightens consciousness; ours, not His. Almost as if in the darkness, we sensed another, near us. It is a sixth sense, this; or a seventh, or eighth. But a sense infinitely more acute, exact, unswerving, than any of the others that stand watch in the body.

The prayer then, indicates where the psalmist stands. It also implies where God stands. And it asks a question: where do you stand? It says: If you would make this prayer, and seek a like hearing, stand somewhere.

A Handful Of Dust Lies In Your Hand / *Psalm 102*

Old, old, flesh rots like a garment
no golden age, no "normal times"
no exit, no return
no sweet bird of youth

One leg, one crutch shuffling the earth
With luck, a friend's strong arm
or a son's or daughter's
and the scarecrow jerks along

Not far. Far as final night.
Breath vanishes on chill air
heart turns to a fist
a fist of clay

How quick the years! a blur,
and they pass, long distance runners

High, wide, handsome our dreams, our youth
we exulted, we mistook
mere vigor for virtue

> *One night's passage, a smoke*
> *a dawn fog,*
> *the portal opens*
> *the stony dead*
> *greet us, blank*
> *eye to eye*

The heavens you set in place
vast, airy
(their cinch pole
like a world's axis)
the great tent rots like a garment!

> *Lord, take the old man in arms*
> *a bag of bones*
> *a newborn child—*
> *have pity*
> *a handful of dust*
> *lies in your hand*

On the one hand, more and more people are surviving into old age. On the other, more and more people are being cut down, far short of old age, short even of maturity. So many prevented from being born, from growing out of infancy. So many stunted, brutalized, shunted aside, offered no place in the world.

And the so-called fortunate ones—those who make it into old age—they inherit and, indeed, help perpetuate a cult of the aged. Dude ranches, senior citizens' clubs, retirement villages, segregated playpens all, futile and trivial attempts to banish the old people, to shelve them, to sweep them out of sight, to convince them that the American dream need never know, this side of eternity—a rude awakening on their part or ours.

In regard to old age, the bible is interesting because it is ambivalent. Age is a natural culmination of goodness or wickedness. In principle, old age is a blessing connected with progeny and an honorable place in the tribe. But, in fact, no false miracles are promised. One grows old in the way one had always walked, no miracles are promised or delivered. A lifelong series of choices lies at the heart of the matter; did one choose for God and others or against them? David grew old, so did Abraham, Isaac—so also Solomon, a different outcome indeed.

In any case, physical decline, loss of vital energies, enfeeblement, all were connected with a view of the world itself. Old age was an image of the decline of high noon in nature; the decline of day toward night, the passage of summer into winter, the banking of the fires of the universe, the tending of all things toward death.

Nothing of this for Christians! They were instructed in a new language, a new reality. New creation, rebirth, healing of limbs; devils cast out, the raising of the dead. Time was turned around, nature was denied or transcended. Human life was granted a second chance, a second birth even. No more death! The cry was an audacious one; more, for a time, it seemed to prevail. The good news was announced to the poor, the jails were sprung, the blind saw, the dead walked again. One has only to read the Acts of the Apostles to gain a savor of the new wine. Here was a community endowed with indomitable youth of spirit, going its own way, against the tide, against opinion, against the threat of criminal punishment, fearless before threats of death, indifferent to comfort or status (indifferent, it seemed at times, to logic itself), working wonders almost methodically, confounding the principalities and powers.

What is the moral equivalent of physical youthfulness? It seems as though Christianity set out to discover the answer, and to demonstrate it. But not, please note, a merely superior ethic, examples of which of course abounded both in Judaism and paganism, when Christianity arose. More than these, by its own claim. Which is to say, a transcendent faith that paid no claim, and little heed, to the overmastering presence of death.

Can Christianity renew itself? Can it turn the tables on the modern world—even on itself? Can it offer to a spiritless age, when the Spirit seems to have flown its own nest, a new spirit?

A matter of uncommon traits, freely offered for the common good:

——Life that is firmly rooted, free in exercise, steadfast in resolve.

——No ululating in the void.

——Ethical alertness, the wisdom that keeps its distance from the world's method and tools.

——Charismatic gifts gratefully received, announced, and passed on to others, in the way of gifts whose giving never ends. Like life itself.

Bless The Lord My Soul
Psalm 104

We have the catalogue by heart
of Your marvels; alas, time stained now
or extinct. We have flogged Your world
to a death sweat, ridden it lame.

Translating David's innocent voice
that struck note by note, the crystalline
forms, plumage, coats of Your world—
no easy task. The note is sour

a gash in the time-riddled throat
of a liberty bell, so called.

It calls the wrong hour, we are abed;
those who cast the fault are long dead

unresponsive, beyond accounting.
Now the priests cry in disarray, you are dead.
A headless god in a sacked temple.
But I will disinter

that dishonored bronze, strike my fist
bloody against its face, if I may
draw from you a last note
that was also the first

that day you plainly uttered the world.
What matter if upstart, mean spirited
we cast in your face the anti-world
a moon dogging your sun?

Sons kill their fathers. Did you enact the law
only to die of it? Listen, despite all—
the world's last day, and we
(your misadventure) and the psalm, end;

Bless the Lord my soul!

They say that in war, the first casualty is the truth. It occurs to me, the times being what they are, the statement leads to another one, analogous to it. When war is the ordinary way of settling human conflict, the first casualty is—God.

In this sense, the Death-of-God faddists of the sixties were perfect grist for the mills of the gods, and as far as they went, were correct. I believe that God dies a little with every murder, every twist of cruelty, every lie, every concession offered to death. He dies in us, he dies in nature, he dies in innocent blood, he dies in a dying universe. His voice is stifled, his holy will mocked, his tenderness set to naught. Vast armaments declare him impotent, vast military budgets prove him insolvent. Pretentious, absurd, sinister beyond belief, modern dictators declare his rule ended.

Somber reflections indeed. And the question occurs to me (indeed, it is pushed at me by a fervent corps of critics): is not this whole line of thought wide of the truth? Are you merely trafficking in misery, refusing to read signs of hope or to grant them place, obsessed and willful, parading out the dark side of existence, peddling this as though it were all of reality? Indeed, if one has a historical sense, have things ever been notably better than they are now? To what el dorado, what mirage do you presume to compare our leadership, our structures, even our church?

The questions are not bad ones. At least they indicate the differing moral worlds people walk in today. The past is invoked with all its violence and turbulence, a corrective against too gloomy a reading of the present. Or the crimes of communists are dwelt on as a way of mitigating our own. (A letter arrived from a Catholic who inquired acidly how I could advocate "wasting our dollars on medical aid to Vietnam." He went on, "You've got the degrees, you've got the brains (purportedly), how come?" It occurred to me that what both he and I need at present is not brains or degrees or dollars. We need the simplest kind of literacy, the ability to read the New Testament: "I was hungry and you fed me. . . . If your enemy strike you on one cheek, turn the other."

I think it is hardly useful to ask: are we better than inquisitors, grand or mini; or are we better than Third Crusaders; or better than witch burners? Or again: are we better than Russians or Chinese in our treatment of political deviants? Who would not grant that we are better? And yet one must insist that better is not yet very good.

Life offers a large space in which savages can be acceptably savage—especially if people have set their sights at absolute zero, taken their moral measurements from the subhuman.

But suppose that instead of starting at Dead Sea level, we raised our eyes to the height of the mount of Beatitudes? The first, I think, implies a great store of cynicism; a blindness that in the world, goes fast and cheap under the guise of realism. The second method begins where God begins—at that improbable height which is still accessible, to which He beckons us, an altitude where humans have access to perspective, breathing space, solitude, vision, and a practical, attainable task.

We do not stand on that height, we do not see our task. We are trying (not really trying) to be superior to Russians or Cubans or Chinese, or someone. And when we have committed a crime, as in Vietnam, our sights are lowered further, in shame. Now we are superior to makers of pogroms, we don't lock dissidents up forever, we are nowhere near as bad as a Hitler or a Torquemada. What a shameful measure for a purportedly civilized people! We are measuring ourselves from beneath, below a moral sea level. In the bear pit, in the race not to be last, in the assault on truth, we entirely lose our bearings.

Which is to say, we die—in our moral life, our sense of one another, our willingness to suffer for justice's sake.

And as these qualities die in us, as death gains the mastery and our despair worsens, we pull down the temple of the universe.

Given the process, God can only be mourned, another casualty in a war declared against reality itself.

But God Is Silent / *Psalm 114*

Sotto voce
cynics pass the word—
Let's hear from your god
How many legions has he?

But God is silent
the creator of splendors

earth and heaven, a dazzle of stars
all creatures that fly, swim, walk,
breathe and blossom
yes and simple unblinking stones
sun and moon, splendid beyond telling
and the squat toad
the owl's myopic stare

This panoply, this outspread
banquet of sight and mind
and its silent
Maker
our momentous Friend
our androgynous Lover!

Logic shall have no more sway. Irrationality rides the world, a breaker of the wild horses of the mind.

The height of irrationality—war, any war. War and the irrational, a harnessed team of hellions; war as the irrational, two poles that merge, two guiding and converging stars of modern polity.

This is why the sardonic ghost of Stalin speaks in the psalm. His Irrational Highness! "The pope, how many legions has he?" Irrationality became Stalin's title of honor, he was morosely proud of his madness, he celebrated it, a mad sword dance. His bellicose consciousness was carried to such lengths that the measure of the human became the measure of the inhuman—in contrariety to history, to his people, to God. His measure, at once lethally simple, a body count to surpass huns and vandals; how many conscript killers at his disposal, how many corpses under his boot.

It is useless to be logical in such situations. Logic has never been notably useful in countering such insanity, curbing such crimes. But other qualities have been—courage, compassion, a sense of humor (even of hangman's humor), motives deeper and loftier than the tyrant can summon.

And then, when the crunch is on and the fist pounds at the door—the presence of grace, a sense of the treasure one carries so precariously, a willingness to sacrifice for its sake. . . .

To counter the high vault of the illogical killer, one must leap very high; even higher than he. That is why during the maddest moments of the Vietnam war, certain noble spirits immolated themselves by fire before the seats of power, the UN, the Pentagon. Their deaths were leaps into high heaven, their illogic turned every eye their way, their cries were heard in every place between earth and sky. They had surpassed the furious and foolish non sequitur of mass killing with their infinitely courageous non sequitur—their own deaths. Thus they confounded the fools in power, by a supreme foolishness, and joined themselves to that folly Paul speaks of, the secret root of all consequent faithful greatness, the folly of the cross.

These thoughts come to mind, as I reflect on this little poem. It celebrates a wrong folly by setting it right. The poem is a folly, illogical. It goes so far as to say that God is foolish, illogical. He has no legions. Or rather, as Jesus put it, He has at His command whole legions of angels; but He will not deploy them, even for His son's sweet sake, for angels, whatever the provocation, are not for killing.

And humans are? And the goods of the earth are? We must go to our deaths saying no.

They Have Idols, A Pantheon Of Idols / *Psalm 115*

Hear the worldlings mock us—
Where is your God?

They have idols, a pantheon of idols!
basilisks, scorpions

satyrs, tri-headed dogs
puppets wired for sound

yes and
arrows and bows, tight strung, true in flight
cannons ranting like mastadons
tight-lipped M-14s

those wooden sticks

touch them—dry as dung
speak to them—ears of stone!

put them to shoulder
they jerk awake
their sights zero in
they bark like dogs
they leap from the leash
their victim lies
asprawl, throat torn.

then
Little Boy, Big Boy
squatting in bunkers   dogs in caves
eyes half closed, jaws
boiling with doomsday juices
their yawn   their bark
makes vincible dust
of the world's sevenfold wonders
And the eumenides spin their thread
as before. The eagles consume
the hero's steaming tripe
as before. The bloody boots
march, crunch as before.

Silent One, silent
as the earth-stopped
mouth of the dead,
silent as the wind-scattered
dust of the children

come to us in the perpetual smog of our discontent

come to us in the fear that clings, a filth, a stench

come to us, half-human, infantile, barely coping

come to us, wanting you, not wanting you, in dread of you.

In our best moments, we want a plain speaking God, a justice dealing God, a peaceable God, one who is visibly on the side of the lowest and least and neediest in our midst. Why doesn't He cry out? We cry out.

Strangely enough, the poem celebrates His . . . silence. Let creation speak for Him, is the implication. Can we object to that? No, we agree, as long as the voice of creation is merely one voice among many, a sotto voce.

Still, can he not now and then, at least once in a human lifetime, speak up loud and clear?

"Now in these latter days, he spoke to us through his son. . . ." A priest I know in Northern Ireland had suffered much at the hands of church and state in that tortured land. Once he said to a group of us: "The first time around didn't seem to help much. Maybe we're supposed to hang on, wait for another coming, I don't know. . . ."

He meant a coming of Jesus different than the second coming, different also than the first coming. Something, some relief, some breakthrough here and now, when so many of us are at the end of our rope, dangling there vertically. An intermediate coming, so to speak; more than the first, not quite the second; a "coming and a half."

I think what the priest spoke of is already underway. It would have to be. Otherwise the world would long ago have gone its own way—to ultimate destruction, a goal fervently embraced, almost from the beginning.

In the book of Genesis we have a clue of how quickly the enterprise of wickedness got underway. Depravity, selfishness, murder built up quite literally to a deluge. And the book of Revelation tells of an ominous beast and its vast human entourage, scouring the earth, stifling all opposition, degrading, reducing all to a mindless herd.

Little comfort is offered to those early times or to our own. Still, we are not left comfortless. The comfort, meager indeed and cold to the touch, is simply the truth; a biblical realism that views human history for what it largely is, views it in its true light, takes into account both crime and punishment.

And offers, beyond the truth and still within it, relief from the truth; crime; but also rebirth, relief.

It is not enough to know our crime, to know that the crime continues, inflates, claims us too. There must be a way out, once responsibility is clarified. It is not enough to say that the Bible has taken into account the social and personal madness that gleams weirdly in public places today. Where shall we go once we are enlightened enough to know, say, the difference between sanity and madness? Is only madness negotiable? Does only madness save? Is God also mad, and are we created in His image?

We take it into account, we freely admit and confess:

——We are malign enough, twisted enough, to bring creation to a smoking ruin.

——We have the instruments.

——We have the myths.

——We even have the blue print.

It is stashed away in some war room, in some hollowed out mountain. It reflects accurately, in lines, graphs, abstract jargon, clean as a rich corpse, the white-lipped love of death that drives us on.

Thus, corresponding to a "second coming," we concoct a "second death," preempting the triumph of Christ, enthroning death in place of the God of life. The throne room is a war room. It is also, one must add, a religious sanctuary. The god is death.

But who will confront this crime, this seizure of creation by demonic tooth and claw?

I think it is only the resisting people. Those who confront weapons, weapons-makers, and their immaculate guardian—the law. And I believe they will prevail. I believe this because I believe in God. The two sentences, in fact, merge within my soul; they are one. If He is God, if a God exists, these are His people. And conversely, if such are the people who declare His existence, I too must believe; I must be one of them, at their side, one voice, one conscience.

They will prevail. Because in them, very nearly all our hope rests. Because in them, goods of mind and heart, neglected squandered human goods, coalesce and survive, shine forth. Citizenship, a sense of humanity, faith untarnished, an unpolluted tradition.

They remind me of an ancient Irish tower I saw standing aloft in Wicklow after some ten centuries. When the alarm sounded in the old villages, I was told, the people withdrew to the tower, taking with them the book and cup. Their tradition, their holy act—these must be salvaged. The barbarians came, pillaged and went. The people withstood.

Such people, today and then, are a kind of Coming-and-a-Half. They are the first coming of Christ spread abroad, very nearly the only good news audible these days. They are not yet his second coming, not by a long shot; as jail is far from honor, courts far from justice, bombs far from bread, cynics far from the truth, power politics from the gospel, the daily news far from the real event. When we pray psalm 115, let us pray for all who clumsily, in weakness, in depression of spirit, far from good repute, still stand somewhere, stand firm, pay up. Come lord Jesus. Keep coming people.

I Love Your Promise / *Psalm 119*

A double heart be far from me, Lord
I love your commands
my hope is your promise

A lying tongue be far from me
I love your promise
my hope is your law

Far from me a violent will
your will is my hope
I love your commands

To witness your law
to love your commands
be my first love.

No one, not God Himself, can command us to love. Nor can we be required, so popular wisdom has it, to love what we are commanded to do. . . .

Yet the psalm, in spite of all, aims to bring the two into consonance—commandment and love. Can this be done?

A great immediate antipathy arises against such an idea. Is it not the essence of love that one is free to embrace or to turn away? Does not the command, love God, love one another, poison the air to the degree that a lover under duress, under orders, is no better than a whore, a pimp of the divine?

I disagree. It seems to me that love is obedient, ringed with a sense of limits, careful not to offend, conscious of taboos, creaturely in fact. It does not go its own way, "do its own thing," in a way precious to the romantic, the immature, the parasitic.

No great sense of history is required to bring the lesson home. Nuclear weaponry puts the future of all humanity in question. (You will pardon me for dwelling in these pages on the Bomb. I feel at times like a half mad Cassandra shouting to a deaf city. I am trying to report a monstrous crime in preparation; the Bomb is within the gates. Very few will listen.)

Yet it is clear that, in this matter, a central law of nature has been violated so grossly that the crime, now seriously contemplated, places authority beyond all human limits, outside creaturely status.

More than this. Can we wonder that, in an age of nuclear abandon, other horrors continually break out—short term losses, local disasters, preludes, so to speak, of the Grand

Act? Pollution, blights, unseasonable storms, shortages of materials, droughts, starvation?

Thou shall love the Lord thy God. . . .

Thou shall not kill. . . .

We had thought the two commands were separable, we had thought each of them negotiable. Plenty of ritual, a brisk business among the money changers, busy altars, a vogue of good works. We would show God what a faithful people looked like! (We would also show Him what He ought to look like.)

We should have known better, we should have read our Bible. One of the earliest stories, a primordial horror, is the murder of a brother by his brother. The killing had the most sinister overtones; it was a quasi-religious act. Abel's offering of first fruits was acceptable to God, Cain's was not. So Cain slew his brother.

We were to learn (we learn by doing) the macabre implications of the story. The murder of brother by brother becomes a wicked stereotype of history. And the religious overtones are never lost; in fact, in every war they break out again, seizing weirdly on the national or tribal soul. Among the nations, bellicose people scan the bible for signs of justification. They ponder those parts that favor their bloody enterprise, they preach, declaim the message. It matters not on which side of the conflict, so-called Christianity can be heard above the guns, blessing this side or that, invoking God on behalf of this or that "just cause." Both sides are just, every war is just. The doctrine vindicates Christianity once and for all, a religion fit to kill. No matter that the God of love issues His command to love Him and one another. Nor that, given our blood lust, cupidity, envy, the command to love God had to be brought down to earth, translated as a prohibition against killing one another. The command to love God is thus tested in our love for one another. A sorry necessity; who would not have thought the connection to be clear by now, war outlawed, men and women getting on with building the earth? Alas, alas.

The command is that we be godlike; that we accept our own humanity under the sign of His, an invitation as gracious as it is stunning; to live by His life, to take our cue from His Spirit, to enter His heart, to share His vision and hope.

The violation of the command, signaled by the warehousing of cosmic mischief, thus has reverberations that stagger the mind. The crime also has religious overtones, overtones that official ears are deaf to. The crime, in religious terms, is nothing less than a mad mime of the crucifixion of God. It would silence, once and for all, that mouth that dares speak of love, commands us to love, gives His life for love of us. Let us have done with such a God, let us prove Him of no account in His world; outmoded, bypassed, irrelevant. We have other gods, hundreds of them, whole pantheons full. Infinitely more powerful than that nonviolent One; their commands set up no conflict, are in full consonance with the dark urgings of our hearts. . . . Hate one another as we have hated you. They command and we obey.

The command to love God also resumes all other commands, a kind of sacred canopy, placing human conduct under the most exalted sign, giving a final dignity to our creaturehood.

If we are also commanded not to kill, not to blaspheme, not to exploit, not to misuse or covet possessions, not to indulge our ego, in lust, in hatred and dissension—all this is a rather spiritless code. Perhaps a code of convenience, or a code of stoics—until the Spirit breathes on it, mothers it. Then, ah then, the commands become the mysterious prelude of a holy visitation, the road the mystics walk.

I love your command! They shout it in exultation.

My Help, My Hope / *Psalm 121*

I lift my eyes to you
my help, my hope

the heavens (who could imagine?)
the earth (only our Lord)
the infinite starry spaces
the world's teeming breadth

All this. I lift my eyes
—upstart, delighted—
and I praise.

God the praiseworthy; this was a constant theme during the liturgical heyday of the fifties.

One is tempted to wonderment in retrospect: what innocents we were, setting up our tents on the volcano's edge. There was something naïve, something inexpressibly moving about us. Children we were, childish even—we had taken so little into account, so little of the past, of our psycho-history, as they say; so much violence was muttering away just below the surface of events, of consciousness. Who could reckon on the storm that was about to break?

And who is to say that in the torrid, bloodshot, nightmarish years since then we have graduated into adulthood? Does innocence always lead to experience? May it not also twist itself into a sour, dispirited stasis, a willful resolve not to learn, not to be compassionate, not to be responsible?

Wherefore, a general statement. No one has been able to demonstrate that Christian worship leads, in any large or direct sense, to Christian conduct in the world. Indeed, if the claim is raised today, we are tempted to say, out of weariness, out of experience, out of the bitter recent past: we have heard all that before.

Indeed, the recent past lies heavy on us. We have seen in modern societies, from Hitler's to our own, liturgies, Christian gatherings, purportedly Christian worship, become the hip, well-tooled, well-orchestrated instruments of fascism, warmaking, glorification of race, "national honor" at any price, platonic ethics made easy ("our misleader, our leader right or wrong").

These reflections are meant to serve a healthy skepticism. Since Vietnam, if not since Germany, Catholics have seen how murder follows on magic, how church silence follows on state lies, how bombings follow on worship, how state and church converge without rising.

In both instances, one might say, real estate is the realest reality of them all.

In reaction against this historical malfeasance, the best are in despair, and the worst in active complicity. Both outcomes, both attitudes strike one as remarkably alike. With this difference, it seems to me, the despairing are generally unaware of the way their inertia serves the powers of death, while the complicit cannot quite conceal the despair they endure, serving the cause they do.

Both are "praising the idols" in the biblical sense. That is to say, they are enlarging the scope of untruth, even as they grant it, practically speaking, life and death power over themselves.

Now and again this situation is dramatized, grotesquely, ludicrously, in public.

A national drama. In late summer, 1976, two American military men are killed while trimming a tree that impeded their view of the enemy, at the South-North Korean border. Whereupon, B-52 bombers, an aircraft carrier, all kinds of lethal hardware is hauled to the scene. Under an ominous umbrella, the tree trimming continues. O that tree of the knowledge of good and evil!

A Christian drama in praise of idols. In the same year, at a huge international convocation purportedly called in honor of the Last Supper of Jesus, a mass in honor of the military is announced. The date is August 6, which at least on a few American calendars commemorates the erasure of a Japanese city. Women, children, men, the old, infants, the ill, beggars and rich, street vendors and merchant princes—all were vaporized in a flash, in the wink of an eye. No matter the sorrowful day, no matter the survivors, the guilty, no matter Jesus—the "mass" was celebrated. A classic example, by no means the first in history, of a black mass, celebrated publicly by the official church. To paraphrase the apostle, where death abounded, death does more abound. The state decrees death, the church celebrates it. In the East this is called yin/yang, or the Ring Around of Mutual Interest.

These are sorrowful words indeed. They are set down here ruefully. I wish I had better things to write concerning a church that is after all, bone of my bone, flesh of my flesh.

I wish with all my heart that the American church were intent on its proper task: praising God, withstanding death. Instead of the opposite.

As The Eyes Of A Lover
Psalm 123

toward you my glance
O Lord of heaven
as the eyes of a son
to his father's hands

as the eyes of a daughter
to her mother's hands
toward you my glance
until you take pity

Take pity Lord—
the high and mighty
make sport of us, mock
the tears they exact—

too long our oppression
too heavy our burden—

as the eyes of a lover
to a lover's hands
toward you my glance
until you take pity

Are we no more than simians, crowned with a cruel hope that forever falls short, a hope more like a curse than a crown?

God our father, our mother, we the sons, we the daughters. Is this a dream, a fabrication designed to keep us hopelessly childish, infested with false hope? Many have said so, with disdain and anger, with despair even, that such a hope, so beautiful, so seductive, should be so untrue.

He has told us. He has spoken first. In spite of all, we take our stand there, on His word. It is a clumsy faith, it has few worldly credentials—fewer still, when it is most itself. (When Christianity is itself, true to itself, it is absolutely unacceptable—intellectually, legally, morally. But at that point that is another story.)

He has told us who He is. There is no question of caviling, of verifying, of asking for signs and wonders. When we do this, we depart from the company of those who *hear*.

I say this with confidence, though I am ignorant as a stone of the consequences. I stretch out my hand, empty as it is, I give that emptiness to Him. He makes much of it, literally.

But He has also told us much about ourselves. If He speaks a word of love to us, it is for the simplest, most astonishing of reasons: because He has loved us first. Before we could choose, we have been chosen. We have been chosen, precisely to enable us to choose, an act that, but for His gift, is as far from our capabilities as bodily flight through the air, or bilocation.

I do not know if such a claim, such a faith, changes the course of the world. Or indeed, if it is meant to. We could certainly nurture a far more bitter complaint against the hand of God had not His son fallen under its blade. "Who did not spare His only son. . . ." The truth steals our thunder, it puts God in our camp, that bloody slave camp into which the world seems bent on transforming itself. It puts Him there, not as torturer or commissar, but as the first victim of all. The fate of God is crueler than the fate of most of us; an argument hard to answer, give up on Him though we do, refuse to trust Him though we do, and most heartily, and for most of our lives.

I do not know what course the world of power and policy, of technology, of tensions, despair, duplicity—what form this would take, what mitigations, what taming of savagery, were His love to become our discipline. Probably the question is an idle one, at least in the sense that no human wisdom can shed much light on it. We know Jesus need not have died, we know the children of My Lai need not have died. We sense, obscurely, a sense that is a deep abiding pain, that we were there, present at both horrors, and at every intervening one, and at whatever ones will follow. We could not stay the hand of Herod; the least we can claim is that his hand is not ours; that his incalculable malice is not a surrogate for our own.

Half-heroes, anti-heroes, half-hearted sons and daughters, echoing faintly or not at all, hiding out, dreading that love which summons us, summons us when all is said, to become ourselves. Which can only be (it sticks in the throat, it sticks in the mind) by choosing . . . to be chosen.

We Died Yet We Live / *Psalm 125*

What if the Lord were silent, unconcerned?
On that day we were lost
Then the world seized us at throat
Then we were cast alive in the flames

The flood all but submerged us
The flames leapt for our throats
In fire and water we went under. We died
yet we live

The fowler's net whispered down
we were helpless as night-blinded birds

Lo, the net is rent like a grave
we are free

Whose eye, whose strength, whose love?

Like night-wakened birds we sing;
Our help is in his name!

What does His silence mean? Or, more precisely, does it have a meaning? Or is the silence of God another way of putting His non-existence, a metaphor drawn from poetry, as one might speak of the silence of a stone? (As though a stone could be anything but silent.)

Here as elsewhere, the psalms seek to awaken imagination and thereby energy, thereby a sense of reality, sanity in fact. They imply: to believe is to imagine God, to imagine that He exists, because in fact He does. The imagination is "after the fact," in a double sense, at least. It follows on the truth of things, it is the servant of reality. But that reality is literally ungraspable by the rational mind (consult the friends of Job for the big mental assault on God; the "now we've finally got him" mentality). So the imagination hovers about the mystery; all it can say is, "It's not this, not that; but it's like this, or like that. . . ." To be imaginative is to be voracious for the truth, to hunger after it; it is the appetite of the soul for the truth. It also means that we respect the truth, by granting it space, by not claiming it intemperately.

The silence of God, a terrifying reality, before which we ourselves had best grow silent. But may one at least suggest this: that when we say God is silent, we say He is being him-

self. When He speaks, it is altogether exceptional. When He acts, it is altogether exceptional. Understood, that is, the way we commonly understand speech and action. As a breaking in on silence, a breakthrough from inaction. Not at all, in His case. His silence is the very intensity of His love; it is all a word, all an act, all a saving deed.

I set these words down, trying to mean them, trying to believe them. I want them to be something more than pious twaddle. I think of those I love, whose lives are, in many cases, a kind of horrific cry of faith, who have borne with much suffering—and who keep on keeping on. No need to list details; everyone has his own life, his own friends, for whom the silence of God, and the mad course of the world, are like an upper and lower millstone. And they are caught between. And the mill grinds on.

This is one unresolved and bloody matter.

Another far different one also occurs to me. It is the matter of a false paradise, from which God is in principle and fact, excluded. I mean by this the institutions of modern life and the aura that surrounds them, the enticements, the sales pitch, the big lie. Perhaps these institutions offer a clue to the silence of God.

Think of those institutions, their growth, their power, their promises; the all-serving, all-promising, all-mighty structures, those robotized, dramatized appetites of ours, on the go for us night and day, on the prowl for us around the world, our armies, navies, air forces, our market hunters, police trainers, foreign investors, our briefcased experts, entrepreneurs, corporate megalomaniacs; that empire of appetites which longs literally to eat the world for its naked lunch. . . . Why, what need of God in our paradise, our perfect environment? Were He to enter, would we not scotch him, as we would a serpent in a garden? Our goods, our services. Our "haves." Our eats and drinks. Our coonskin on the wall. For these and all other benefits, we render thanks—to ourselves.

What need of God? What need in so perfect a world, for the Imperfect Mystery?

What Marvels The Lord Works For Them / *Psalm 126*

When the Spirit struck us free
we could scarcely believe it
for very joy. Were we free
were we wrapt
in a dream of freedom?
Our mouths filled with laughter
our tongues with pure joy.

The oppressors were awestruck; What marvels
the Lord works for them!
Like a torrent in flood
our people streamed out.
Locks, bars, gulags, ghettoes, cages, cuffs
a nightmare scattered

We trod the long furrow
slaves, sowing in tears.
A lightning bolt loosed us.
We tread the long furrow
half drunk with joy
staggering, the golden
sheaves in our arms.

For many of my friends this psalm will have a familiar ring. For the prisoners and the ex-prisoners; for the random unlucky or prematurely conscientious or plucked and chastened; for the guilty and the innocent, the far and near, the countless souls on ice, or under a spring thaw. To all of them, the poem speaks of a moment beyond all moments. Freedom! The moment that is always there, tantalizing, untouchable, distant but visible, a star you lifted your hand to in salute, set your sights by, crossed out calendar dates by.

The moment that would never arrive! It was madly improbable, the frown of a brute could wipe it out of the sky. It danced cruelly, surreally on the walls, tracing a graffito; not yet, not yet. It whispered in your dreams. Then it fell to your hand. You were free!

Let us pray this psalm for the thousands of prisoners who will never taste such a moment. In Chile, Paraguay, Uruguay, Argentina; in South Korea, the Philippines, Vietnam; in India and Pakistan and Iran; in Uganda and Kenya; in Spain, Ireland, Lebanon, Israel; in southern Africa and Rhodesia and Namibia. These countries and so many more; really in every regime under the sun, left, right, centrist; since in all countries, to greater or lesser degree (but always to some degree), the real crime is conscience, the prospect is prison; more often than not, the nightmare is torture.

Let us pray the psalm; those who have never paid its price, stood at its far end longingly, looking through bars, waiting, hoping. In order that those who pay so heavy a price may know some reward—fearlessness, patience, courage, even exaltation of heart.

A strange prayer, that a prisoner's heart may lift in ecstasy? Let me only say, I have tasted it. It came unannounced, undeserved, in the midst of a Buddhist austerity which is also celebrated in the Gospel: blessed are the poor in spirit . . . blessed those who suffer persecution for justice's sake.

Kim Chi Ha, a Korean poet frequently tried and tortured for his crimes of the pen, for poetry celebrating his faith and satirizing tyrants, has tasted this pure joy. Even under torture, pushed to extremes, at one point condemned to death, he writes like an ecstatic.

Let us pray that the Spirit offer to prisoners a gift the jailers can never snatch from them.

And The Lord Enters / *Psalm 127*

There goes the money maker, ant
in an ant hill, frantic,
zooming, cannonading
See the glint in his eye

Dawn, he's up
like a shot; dark, he's daylight
saving. That puritan ethic
is cold energy. Time's money
his thin lips count it, clock it.

Imagine
his family; sons and daughters

items on a ledger.

And the Lord enters like termites
serpentine, miles, a rope, a whisper
a noose, bad news.

The great house
shifts in sleep, dry bones.

I must take responsibility for this poem, not David. (Though I hope it is in his spirit.) I wrote it because I live where I do—amid the wrecks, the hungry, the stoned, the drifters and drunks of upper Broadway. Because I live among beggars and shopping bag ladies, and those who bed down in the streets. Because I live among destroyers: those who wreck a beautiful neighborhood, rob stores, mug pedestrians, stalk the old and helpless, piss drunkenly on sidewalks, sit amid their own garbage and debris, rotten kings on a dung heap. You can find me, one mile distant as the crow flies from the million dollar penthouses of Fifth Avenue, three miles north of the twin World Trade Towers, a bit further from Wall Street. To the northeast of us things are worse: Harlem. And ten blocks due north, presto, another world, the crew-cut, guarded acres of Columbia.

I dread it, loathe it, love it. I rage, things should not fall apart this way. I am sick of danger, violence, black looks, drunks and pimps, pushers, dealers, hookers.

They say there is no help for us, no money. The banks own the city, the mayor and governor take orders from Chase Manhattan, the other silk-suited suavities. I think this is true; New York is undergoing the first bloodless coup of a great city in my lifetime.

I was in Hanoi during the most brutal bombing attacks, those of Johnson in '68. I have never seen a bomber over Manhattan. But we have been bombed, we have capitulated. To no foreign enemy; in fact to no "enemy" at all. The sword of money is at our throat.

This is a terrifying anti-gospel drama. Gospel, and anti-gospel. Gospel, because it has been predicted, warned of. Anti-gospel, because anti-human; the sword of money is pointed at the throats of the poor.

I do not know enough history to be comforted by the old sop of the experts: "all this has happened before." I am terrified, astounded. I see the book of Revelation being acted out before my eyes. You have to see it, verse by verse, the fall of Babylon before your eyes, to believe it. A stupendous fall, the end of something, a truth we knew only as a theory, something heard in sermons, read somewhere in the Gospel: you cannot serve God and money. The outcome is the fate of my city.

You can try this double service of course, right hand and left, the ambi-dextrous conscience, the wink, the gift under the table. Almost everyone tries it, one way or another. Then quickly or slowly (it doesn't matter) a transformation gets under way, the dream embraces the outcome—one ends by serving the god, Money. (You see, the upper and lower cases are exchanged: god, Money.) The sale is final.

And the market is bullish. New York may be dying, but the bull pen is bellowing.

It is worth remarking that the banks feel no pinch, nor do the wealthy, who learn on the way up to stay up. No pinch, one must add, at the Pentagon.

I hesitate to say that such skills, followed by such rewards, are a merely human arrangement. I think they are an idolatrous arrangement; it seems to me, further, that when Christ declares that a dual arrangement of gods will not work, he neglects to say (though he indeed implies) what will work. That is to say, a single arrangement—either One God, or one god.

Now we might conclude that being who he is, he is conscious only of the arrangement we might call the truthful one, the one that corresponds to reality. That is to say: worship of the Father in spirit and truth. We neglect the thought that, being who he is, he is conscious also of something else: the fortunate, well oiled, enviable arrangement whereby the god Money is invoked, honored, worshiped, thanked. And how well that god rewards!

Interesting. Jesus did not say: you cannot serve money. The statement, even from him, would be contrary to fact. As an imperative, it would have been contradictory; as well forbid the world to turn on its axis! There was no point in forbidding that enterprise, which is the quintessential enterprise of the world itself, universal, inevitable, roughly comparable to the turn of the tides, the law of gravity and other like phenomena.

No, he was presumably speaking to believers, to whom might occur the friction of a divided mind. In their secret minds, he may have sensed a debate in progress, a dialogue with god Money; why not try me? But there is as yet no question of a pact concluded, an inner shrine already erected (doing business, as they say). Otherwise why would he insist that we refuse to sign the pact, refuse to erect the shrine?

How can we tell if our service is turning away from true God to the god Money? I conclude with a suggestion to those of troubled mind. I think there is a way of telling, in America, today.

It seems to me that slavery to Money, the deification of Money, is connected, by an umbilical of whipcord and steel, to the deification of Death. One notes this in every presidential campaign. There is an all but unmentionable area, off limits to debate: the military. The candidates are like two princely renaissance rogues, vying for the favor of a local saint. One rogue wants to "go all out," as they say; cover the basilica with gold leaf, let a kind of extravagant awe be the irrefutable sign of our devotion. The other, a bit more cautious, reminds his subjects mildly that the saint's holy place is also honored by attention to other matters. He makes it "absolutely clear" that he yields to no one in his devotion; he will keep the shrine in tiptop condition, foster pilgrimages, respect and reward the temple high priesthood. But he would for the present withhold the gold leaf project until further studies are made. Meantime, his mind is open on the matter.

So charming an image, of course, can no longer be a local one. We are an empire; it is only fitting that the little *santo* of the story grow and grow til, like us, it bestrides the world. Except that this demi-god also bestrides us. His name is Death. His shrine must be the finest, his instruments most skilled, his empery like ours, always expanding. He must be paid offerings of food and drink; he is a voracious god, a cannibal. (It may be discovered one day that the priests are secretly eating the human flesh left at his shrine. But that is a scene of judgment too distant, too tempting, to dwell upon.)

It remains that the military is eating us alive—cannibalism. It remains that there is a duty here for Christians who worship a different God indeed. Rather than take our flesh, he offers us his own. "My body, given for you."

I reflect as I write this, there must have come into the troubled reflections of German Catholics, some forty years ago, thoughts like these. Are we not required to withdraw our money from Hitler's war machine; and thereby our complicity with his crimes?

There will be innocent Americans in the years ahead, and criminal Americans. The first will be in great trouble with the law of the land, the others will walk abroad without challenge, hold jobs, raise families. And pay taxes. And worship: Mars, whose other name is Money. They will have resolved the double mind dealt with by Christ. In hell there are no double minds.

I Take My Stand On His Word
Psalm 130

Out of the depths I cry to you, Lord
Lord hear my voice
be attentive to my cry

If you remember our sin
who could bear it?
No, your glory is your forgiveness

My soul hopes in the Lord
I take my stand on his word
More than the sleepless awaiting the dawn
my soul awaits him

As a vigiler awaits the dawn
let his friends await the Lord

For with him is grace in abundance!
Out of the depths
I take my stand on his word.

I think of this psalm as though it were written on a great diamond. Or its words were incised on crystal, hard, cold, perfect. Or the figures—man, woman, God—were worked in enamel in clear opaque colors; in any case, no chiroscuro, no shadows; a portrayal of the human situation, as though an inspired child had seen it once for all. Things are this way, no hiding our tears. We are in the depths, why not declare it?

Our friend, our sufferer, our brother and sister, cries out. And this is part of the perfection, this cry, which the crystal or enamel could not capture, except by implication, an expression, a look in the eye, a godlike hand extended from above, from a cloud. But the psalm gives us the cry.

Upon that cry I think our whole life depends. Not only in the sense that, unless it is uttered, we draw no attention, win no hearing. I mean something else too. The cry to me is the "unwobbling pivot" of what was else only a work in enamel, an incised jewel, a still life. And what kind of life is that?

No, the cry is the sign of existence, the seal of our humanity. Enraged, half-choked, a mere murmur, a blood curdling twist, a kind of prayer even, a sigh of resignation, acceptance, its form seems to me secondary. But when the cry is uttered, the person is named. It is as though a seed had sprouted in a lunar waste.

We are in the depths, granted. But do not beasts also fall into ditches? It is the cry that is all the difference.

The cry—to another. Not a cry in the void. Nor a cry to another, like ourself, trapped in the depths.

A cry to God. This I find beautiful, moving beyond words. This I find the signet upon our humanity, a faith that is under duress, that is required in the world to taste its own tears.

But a faith, not a mere fate. Therefore, not only the world, but a life; not only the problematic, the labyrinth, but the mystery. Not a cul de sac, but a way, both in and out.

I confess I do not know how I could exist for an hour bereft of this ornament, this light around the body, this epiphany of my humanity, which seems to me all that keeps me aglow, not a burnt out case. I cannot even put myself in the position of one who found the cry of this psalm incomprehensible—an empty word hurled in the void. My imagination is too limited, I cannot describe to myself, let alone to others, what it would be like not to believe, and yet to be where I am, in the depths.

That is to say, as I sense my situation, a totally unadapted fish who finds himself plunged literally out of his depth; as to pressure, intense, as to light, meager, as to sustenance, hard come by. And dwelling there, troubled, tons of water per square inch which is the mad weight of life today, of ruinous leadership, of a violent tug and slide of all things toward ruin, of the necessity (almost as the Greeks saw it, a personage, a stony-eyed goddess) of putting off projects, good work, because the times are not merely inopportune, but plain mad. The weight also of seeing the noble consciences of friends driving them to the wall, and behind it, when in sane circumstances they and I could be building, not resisting. This is what I mean by the depths. We were not made for them, and we must dwell in them. We were made to build churches, to succor the poor, to see the fruit of our hands, the very proof and good sense of life manifest to us, as in other ages, men and women surveyed their life, saw "that it was good."

You see the psalmist plunged there, into the depths. But he rose again, he swam near the surface, breathed easier. The psalm was a mood, a killing mood, a cry of anguish. But then the mood altered, the cry was forgotten, there are other psalms, lesser depths.

But I think, with us, the cry is frozen, it is forever. That is why I think of it as a stroke of acid along the crystal, issuing from the human mouth, a line of words toward the hand of God. The cry is part of me, as my mouth is, or the face I raise to Him. The cry is long, long as the distance from those depths to His infinite heights. It is as long as life itself, a lifeline. Or it is a hooked line; maybe we are drawn out of the depths by that hand pulling on that line; we die of that terrible weapon, but we are drawn upward too. At least I hope so. I take my stand on His word.

May I To My Lord Hasten
Psalm 131

Lord cut my cloth
to a human measure—
big schemes, big follies
the dark ground of connivance
be far from me

Come my soul
like a bird to the hand
like a child to breast
I will nurture you, mother you

As my soul hastens
to breast, to hand
may I to my Lord
hasten. Abide.

I hope that someday, someone will set this little poem to music. The music I think, should be modest, in accord with the virtue the poem celebrates.

Camus asks, in one of his novels, why the plague struck the people of the city. Someone answers: they forgot to be modest, that is all.

I've thought of that for years. No explanation is granted; Camus leaves it at that. No explanation is needed? I'm not sure.

Anyway, in that immodest year, 1976, celebrating an immodest bicentennial, whose myths are not only immodest but obscene, not only bigger than life but devoid of life, not only untruthful but lethal—in such a time and place, I grew more than ordinarily grateful for this prayer, this modest request modestly stated.

It is not I think that one is asking God to cut us off at the knees, but perhaps to topple us off our absurd stilts, where we strut along like circus characters—absurd, that is, to everyone but ourselves.

I like the tone of the poem; it is warm, cherishing. A kind of nesting song, as though one's first love ought to be oneself, as long as that beloved is not also the one, only and last love as well. Then the nest is indeed befouled, and the song awry.

Hand In Hand, Heart In Heart
Psalm 133

Sisters and brothers dwell in peace
What joy, what an omen!
Hand in hand, heart in heart
a double strength

A waterfall pausing, various, ever moving,
roses, surprising strawberries
A closed circle, an enclosed garden, a universe—

There
war's hoarse throat is silenced
and praise goes up night and day
and the stanchions of slaves in the hills
gather dust, spring ivy.

We await the ideal community, as we await our own coming of age, coming of height, coming of breadth, coming of—love.

Necessarily a matter of the future, with that terrible necessity which sin imposes, and the heavy hand of death. A necessity that lies at the heart of things, which is a heart of darkness. A necessary future—what a phrase!—expressing as it does a law of sin, a domination that curses the temporal with forever falling short. Short of an act of God.

And yet, and yet, a great hope dawns. That act of God, that promise, is of such power, such unassailable purpose, that it continually casts across the path of history, hints, beckonings, signs, echoes, a memory never lost, a future always nearing, a shadow all of light.

Not as though we were the measure of that future; as though its consummation drew near because of the seductive power of our goodness over the heart of God. No, He is too austere for that, too aware of our true measure, too much Himself. Too jealous, scripture says. When He comes, He will come because He comes; which is to say, because He is God, and therefore pure gift. Nothing can be found in us, either today or on that day, which declares to him: now you owe them at length that they come of age, come of height, come of breadth, come of love.

Yet there is something that draws him. It is what draws the saint to the leper, it is the sleepless love of a mother for a fretful, feverish child. If He comes to us, a hint lies in that very necessity which binds us hand and foot, tongue and brain, conscience and heart. That we cannot be ourselves apart from Him, that we traffic in the bestial, that the march of history is by and large the march of tyrants, sycophants, prisoners, slaves, brutal winners, distempered losers—distempered losers becoming brutal winners. That nothing changes, that we are linked mile upon mile, eon upon eon in that slavish procession, a cacophany of misery; that while some die at the rear of the march (die in chains), others are born up ahead—born in chains. But nothing changes.

And yet, we suggested, there are signs, hopes, something different, some possibility always declaring itself. Among these, the community, the community of the promise. A community governed not by necessity or by a pure future, a future as bound by necessity as the past or the present. Governed by an ethic of the promise. By His will for humanity; therefore free, embodied, here and now. Love one another, as I have loved you.

It seems important to stress that such communities, rare as they are when they are genuine, are not mere cultural counterfeits. The counter culture is not the promise; it is as far from the promise as the culture is. Though it may indeed have attained a measure of peaceableness, unity of outlook, common purpose, these more often than not are signs of a certain refined selfishness, a search for the good life among the ruins, a more humanistic path than that worn bare by the common march. A more skillful way, in the end time of a worn out culture, of extracting the last thin juices of an exhausted fruit. A stirrup cup to extinction.

What is lacking here is a counter sign, a keen edge, a quality of over-against. Communities of faith; they do not live on the presumption that a bend in the path will reveal the rainbow, its buried treasure. The image is a childish one in any case, rather than a Christian one. The coming of Christ will not be a "better future made present;" it is a break with all possible futures, therefore, inevitably, with the present. It is a break with death, a breaking of the lethal covenant. It is a break with death as social method, as military method, as racism, as war, as payment of war taxes, as consumerism, as cannibalism.

It is impossible to respect a community today that does not have this edge to it, this acute sense of the demonic at large in the world, a sense of the boot at the door, the mailed fist knocking, the claim of death. We cannot live as though the world were not the world, that is to say the kingdom which enthrones death as lord and master; we cannot live as though America were not America—and still claim to be Christian. Is this a cliché? Cliché or not, it is a sentiment honored universally—in the breach.

Still, in spite of all, the different drummer must not cease beating out a different march. Among the living, it is the beat of one's very heart.

The procession that forms around the drummer may be rag tag and rebellious, clumsy, out of step. We need to be reminded (the churches almost never remind us) the kingdom is also out of step with the world; compared with the lethal purring of the fat cats, with their cheshire smile (which never deserts them, though Rusk may go and Kissinger come)—to such, the kingdom must appear rebellious, clumsy, laughable even. No matter, in a criminal time, these are not faults. They are precious signs of reality, of survival, of a nearly self-extinguished humanity. Let the one who can hear, fall in.

Lord You Know Me Through And Through / *Psalm 139*

Lord you know me through and through
you take soundings
you pierce my thought
you shadow me, set me alight

A word is scarcely on my tongue
half-formed, a half-savored food—
you know it a to z
you pluck it before it falls

How then flee you, heaven's hound?
hell's falcon, how put you off?
outer space, inner; no contest

In fantasy I take wings
like the boy Icarus, flee you—
land's crush, sea's claw
At verge of pure nothing
pure vertigo
I fall
to your fowler's net

No escape.
"No exit" is your name
via purgativa, fire and sword
your method

My madness, my method
how well I know it—
despair, gross fatalism
the carnal indentured dance
a mask of hell self-fused

A lethal litany!
beyond
its fits and starts
its half a heart

hear my prayer!

Life giver, life's Lord
show me your way!

The thought strikes me: what an astonishingly modern prayer! The prayer of an anti-hero.

The double mind; split, each half in a double bind. Courageous and afraid, faithful and faithless, taking soundings in the universe, incurably curious, self-aware, his knowledge both exalting and punishing. Seeking out and sought after, one step forward, two steps back; inflating God in order to deflate himself, deprecating, self-mocking; and yet, the ego on parade, self-stroking: see me, how lowly I am (and proud of it).

I love someone who can pray this way; there is a kind of dance to it, many rhythms, many facets, complex. Like the Hopi ceremonies, performed half below ground, half above; a secret discipline, and a public one, the conscious, the unconscious, things hidden, things revealed. Part of life's act goes on in the sight of all; but there is also the flight to the "kiva," our roots go down and down; we have dark beginnings, and must return; must come from somewhere if we are to go somewhere.

But the prayer is much more than a celebration of the modern spirit. Indeed it evokes it, only to break with it. And in several respects, it seems to me.

There is a flight understood in radically different ways. According to the psalmist, pure dread, dread of penetration by the Unknown, the All-knowing. Flight from reality. Flight also from himself; his plight, alienation, free-floating anxiety. He would prefer to flee to somewhere dark at the northern or southern pole, in winter, not knowing himself, unknown by that mysterious hounding Other. Alas, his season is wrong, the sun was there ahead of him.

Always that hovering sense of the Other, a shadow on the mind, relief and burden both.

There is another kind of flight, undertaken in a totally different spirit, the modern spirit. Airborne, then ether borne, then space borne. Also a testing of the limits, a risk of disappearing around that infinite curve of nothing. The journey without, pure outside, a bending away forever. A flight without insight. A pure extension of ego; they planted a flag on the moon, and a placque extolling the feat. Pride has a long reach, we now presumably have annexed a 51st state. Shall we call it the Plain of Absurdity, skirted by a dry lake, crowned by a dead volcano? Dead, dry, airless, the end of our journey, as near nothing as one can get.

There are flights and flights. Some end in wisdom, a bitter wisdom; some in folly, a prideful folly. It seems to me the psalm prefers the former flight, and thus prefers a bitter wisdom to a prideful folly. This is the break with the modern spirit, the point of departure. A prayer, a sense of creaturehood, a cry for help.

And more. There is something chastening, something that gives pause, in the belief that these psalms are a kind of duet, a point and counterpoint; better, a double voice merging. My mind returns again and again to this mysterious interplay, so co-penetrating that one would be foolish indeed to try and separate out the voices; this one of God, this of

David. In any case, why try? Why cannot the prayer be totally God's and totally David's, teacher and teachable one, friend and friend, loving adversary each to the other?

In such a case (which I believe to be a more fruitful way), one thinks not only of how David sees himself as "opposite" God, but the reverse as well—how God sees himself as "opposite" David, the flight and the end of flight, the dread and the healing of dread.

To each the other. Each to the other. David is incomprehensible (first of all to himself) without God. Hence the flight, resistance, wrestling, anguish, the necessary bondage, the freedom shout. He must battle that which he loves—because he loves.

And on God's side, the voice of the other, its power to move His heart. A gracious God who will not give Himself cheaply, but at great cost; as His son showed in his blood. Hence He is not, cannot be, to this man David a kind of afterthought, a convenience or prop, a genie, a servant of appetite. The prayer is filled, you must see, not only with the affright of David. Read there also the agony of God. Our world. Ourselves.

It is in such matters I find the poem breaking with the modern mind. Simplest put, because of a prayer, and a kind of flight, and its ending; airy, tearful, fiery; enough passion to burn up the flag on the moon, to stoke its dead mountains, water its deserts. Which are, after all, a lunar image of ourselves, without God, dead fires, deserts, the absurd idolatrous flag.

I Praise, I Exalt Your Name
Psalm 146

I praise, I exalt your Name!

Shadow and Light
Absent One
Tragic Encroacher

half my soul You are
Teaser, Enticer
Ecstatic One,
Fury and Fury's Abater
Breath of the Whirlwind
Breath of the Lover

The earth is your evidence, stars and high heaven

prophetic seas, jeremiads
dark voweled from their lips

truth is your citadel
and justice
and bread for the parched
and chains struck off
sight for the blinded
Haven and hand are you
to the road-ridden wanderer

Such is the God of his people!

A simple song of praise. To enlarge upon it would be awry, all wrong. I write this on a cliff, over the sea. The sea traces a horizon, clearly, strongly, like the line of a Chinese brush on a scroll. The high hill twists like a serpent's middle body, into a lower hill, just in front of this house. An ominous sign this break, an open wound; from it vegetation, boulders, fall in the sea, the cliff inches toward the house, its scruffy head upstanding like a beast's. Ships big and small move modestly about their business, all the time in the world. You would think a child pushed them gently along in a tub of water, or let them be. As if only cruise ships existed; fishing, oil, cargoes, port of call, huff and puff, all forgotten. The sea exists this morning to be looked at; simple as that. All ships at sea are only for my pleasure.

The fields are aglow, golden in vesture, silver on reflection; like a sun looking at itself, in a burnished shield, praising itself. Blackberries, rose hips, are all harvested, or fallen. The way back, the great cycle is underway, another turn of the wheel.

Crows are on patrol; they bicker away on outlying bushes; an elder issues noisy directions; no one pays any attention. They are cruel, scrambled, strong of ego, mean of eyes; they look even on this sunny imperial day, like original sin on the wing. Caw caw, they mock and traduce.

A golden hawk shoots by in the narrow enclave between cliff and sea. Like a thrown knife. Something, beware!

Everything in place, everything in movement, everything alive. The island sits on the sea like an anemone, a universe, dragonflies to hawks to reindeer, splendid bird brained pheasants, swans riding the island waters as the island rides the great sea, and the earth its ocean of space. World within world within world!

Praise Him.

Afterword

Thus have I heard: the Exalted One was once staying in a cave near Savatthi with Ananda his beloved disciple. It was a beautiful morning, and while Ananda was watching the blue horizon he saw a cloud of smoke appearing in the sky. No time had passed at all before he saw standing in front of him Mara, the king of the demons.

What are you here for, Ananda asked.

I want to see Lord Buddha.

Go away Mara, Lord Buddha will not see you.

Why?

Don't you remember that nearly 2,600 years ago you were defeated by Him under the Bodhi tree? Don't you have any sense of shame? You are our enemy, not our friend, and we do not want to talk to you.

As I see it, you are not a good disciple of Gotama, Mara smiled at Ananda. Should a Buddha discriminate between friends and enemies? Does He need to have an enemy?

The Venerable Ananda felt embarrassed. He went in the cave to inform the Lord about the visit of Mara. The Enlightened One came out of the cave and smilingly invited Mara in, as if he were one of His closest friends.

When they had sat down, Mara said: This disciple of yours did not let me in. I had to use a trick. Lord Buddha told Mara: Using tricks is your way. Otherwise you will not be qualified as Mara. Thereupon, Mara complained to the Enlightened One: I am tired of being Mara. All day talking in Mara language, dressed in Mara clothes, behaving in Mara manner. Trying to make everything look dark, hopeless, deceitful, tricky. I am really tired of being Mara, oh Gotama.

The Enlightened One told Mara quietly: You would not enjoy being a Buddha either. You will have too many disciples to be responsible for. You will have too many temples to live in although what you need is a cave. You will be depicted in white, in bronze, in black, in grey, in saffron, even in gold and silver. You will have to sit still all day and all night in a lotus or half lotus position. When they no longer need you, they smash you. You and your teachings will become an object of trading. By your own disciples. You better remain what you are supposed to be, Mara.

My entire army of demons and imps all feel like me now. My people want a revolution. And I understand them. I hear them speak of wisdom, of compassion.

It would sound strange for demons to speak of wisdom and compassion, the Enlightened One remarked. It just does not sound right.

But your disciples speak *too much* of wisdom and of compassion too, don't they, Mara protested. That angered my people. Do you think that mine have the right to speak about wisdom and compassion too?

I guess everyone has the right to do so, Mara, the Enlightened One conceded. Then Mara burst out laughing: There is a bit of trouble, Lord. Twenty-six hundred years ago, there was a tacit agreement between us that your side stands for wisdom and compassion, and mine for ignorance and hatred. Now since the demons want to speak of wisdom and compassion, my leadership is no longer needed. You should take my people over, Gotama, and I shall have a long, beautiful retreat.

Mara, you should not think that that was an agreement made 2,600 years ago. Somewhere in my teaching it was said that dharmas are neither defiled nor immaculate. The good fighting the evil was just a figure of speech. You took it too literally, and my people took it too literally.

But you are too idealistic, Lord. How could people fight evil if they do not believe that evil exists? You do not seem to know that people will not be able to survive if they find no evil to fight. And by fighting they make each other suffer. They want to believe that they are making the evil suffer.

It is better not to fight evil than to fight it and have to kill people.

No wonder they call your teaching the opium of the people, Gotama. People of our times need to fight evil more than in any other time. If they find no evil to fight, they will have to invent it. They point to something, call it evil, call it the enemy, create a feeling of fear and hatred for it, and fight. Many "civilizations" have been founded on this kind of fighting. Your teaching, Gotama, has also been described as a fight between Prajna (wisdom) and Avidya (ignorance). You will tell me that according to your teaching, reality transcends all concepts of quality such as one and many, good and evil, nirvana and samsara, etc. But who will understand this? Take a look at Ananda, this disciple of yours who has been standing there since the beginning of our conversation. He was quite sure that I am your worst enemy. And he has practiced your dharma over 2,500 years. Everyone wants a side to take. No one wants a no-side teaching.

What do you have to propose, Mara?

I am confused, Gotama. And this is natural, because I am supposed to be the Confused One. You will have to ask your Enlightened Self. You always say: Fight the evil and spare man. But it is hardly possible to separate man from his evil. Evil is not a disease that can be removed from a human body. Evil in many is like evil in nature. Wind, water and heat, in the case of natural disasters (catastrophes), are evil themselves. Can you not spare them if you want to remove disasters?

Do I need to tell you, Mara, that there are ways of preventing, controlling and healing, the Enlightened One asked.

Are you speaking of the establishment of a "just system" or are you just speaking of the emancipation of individuals? I know that you will say "both." I want to know whether a "system" can really come to existence if it refuses to fight evil, the kind of evil that can only be found outside of that system. To build a system, one needs a good cause. And one gets a good cause by opposing all the bad causes, evil.

You are playing your role well, Mara. People still need

confusion. A lot of people are still too sure of themselves. Then the Lord turned to Ananda and continued: You know, O Ananda, that right action is the same as right view. Actions are obstacles to action. Views are obstacles to view. Listen to what I have to say. Then the Exalted One recited the following stanza to Ananda:

This is because that is; this is not because that is not.
A Mara is because a Tathagatha is.
A Tathagatha is an obstacle for seeing a Tathagatha.
A Mara is an obstacle for seeing a Mara.
Prajna is Avidya, because without Avidya, Prajna cannot be attained.
Avidya is Prajna, because without Prajna, Avidya has no role to play.

Once the good is removed, the evil ceases to exist.
Once the evil is removed, the good need not to be proclaimed.
The fight ends before it has a chance to start.
Action should begin with a smile; non-action should also begin with a smile.
The obstacle for action is not non-action; the obstacle for action is action itself.
Those who seek for the Tathagatha will never see the Tathagatha.

The conversation between Lord Buddha and Mara went on. But Crossroad Books only wants three pages; so Ananda is glad to stop here. Another day, perhaps.

THICH NHAT HANH